OUT OF TOWN
SHOPPING

THE FUTURE OF RETAILING

By PHIL RUSTON

THE BRITISH LIBRARY

Out of Town Shopping: the future of retailing
ISBN 0-7123-0848-2

Published by:
The British Library
96 Euston Road
London
NW1 2DB

British Library Cataloguing-in-Publication Data
A catalogue record for this book is available from The British Library.

Desktop publishing by Concerto, Leighton Buzzard, Bedfordshire.
Tel: 01525 378757

Printed in Great Britain by Atheneum Press Ltd, Gateshead, Tyne and Wear.

For further information on science, technology and business titles contact
Paul Wilson on 0171-412 7472.

Contents

Introduction

It is now ten years since David Kirby compiled the reference source *Shopping in the Eighties*.[1] At the time of its publication the retail industry was sizable but only just beginning to show the signs of becoming the giant it is today. Almost 10% of the UK's working population are now involved in selling goods to consumers in Europe's fourth largest consumer market. The retail sector in Britain accounts for almost 40% of all consumer expenditure and is worth an estimated £143 billion a year. The 300,000 people employed in the retail trade are operating upon approximately 37 million square feet of sales space. Tesco has around 9 million customers a week, one-fifth of the population of the UK. Everyone is consumed by shopping. It permeates all our lives. The BBC has recently screened a docu-soap based at Lakeside, the large out-of-town shopping centre situated off the M25 in Essex. It has also run a series called 'Shop 'Til You Drop', which looked at the psychology of shopping. The series investigated a "whole new science, the anthropology of the aisles." As Mark Souhami, chairman of the British Retail Consortium, has said, "the (retail) industry is dynamic and there is no doubt that the competitive nature of the market, combined with the creative nature of retailers, has transformed the quality of life in Britain." There can be no disputing the fact that retailing in the 1990s is big business.

In 1987 the possibility of online shopping was a pipe-dream for all but a few mail order companies. Today, the arrival of the Internet has meant that home shopping via a computer terminal has become a reality for many consumers. The impact of new technology will continue to have a major impact on our shopping habits. Sociologists concerned at the deterioration of local communities due to the advent of out-of-town retailing may well see events travel full circle as consumers look to local stores in order to complement their home shopping sprees. The market for online shopping will grow to around £4 billion worldwide within the next two years. This is still only a fraction of the amount we spend through more conventional means, but online shopping will offer much greater margins for retailers since it enables them to sell direct, without expensive middle men, and to tailor stock levels to demand more accurately than is possible through a normal supply chain. The retail revolution is moving from the high street via out-of-town shopping centres to the information superhighway. Just as the growth of out-of-town retailing has left its mark on the high street, the trend towards electronic commerce will alter lifestyles even further. Names such as Tesco, Sainsbury's, Argos, Waterstones, and Interflora are among British retailers rising to the challenge and offering their products through sites on the World Wide Web. Banks, estate agents, travel agents, airlines, and retailers are appearing on the Web, some initially just displaying information and others already selling online.

This *guide* to the literature will lead the reader through every aspect of retailing, from the social and environmental aspects inherent in out-of-town development and the diminution of the high street to the brave new world of electronic commerce.We start by looking at the debate of out-of-town vs. high street shopping, something which has continued to the fore despite a change in government.As recently as September 1998 a government research report claimed that large out-of-town supermarkets were taking up to half the market in small towns and district centres and forcing many food shops to close, with devastating effects on small market towns. The net result was described as "a general decline in the quality of the environment of the centre." The Department of the Environment, Transport and the Regions said the report, produced by CB Hillier Parker, justified its policy of concentrating new superstores in existing centres and resisting new out-of-town developments. Richard Caborn, minister for the Regions, Regeneration and Planning, told the Action for Market Towns conference in Shropshire the report "firmly establishes that out-of-town superstores can seriously damage the health of small towns and district centres."[2] He urged local planning authorities to get their plans up to date and identify the town centre sites where new shopping development should be encouraged. "Planning has got to change from being reactive and negative to being positive and proactive. The only way to get development where you want it is to plan for it," he said.

The government report was published only days after a report prepared for the Office of Fair Trading (OFT) said that the big savings made by supermarkets tended to enhance company profits rather than be passed on to customers. Economists from Loughborough, Warwick and Nottingham universities told the OFT that supermarkets may be abusing their huge buying power. Practices they identified included charging "slotting allowances" – where food manufacturers have to pay to get their goods put on the shelves. The academics said food manufacturers can be further squeezed by supermarkets threatening to take goods off their shelves if the manufacturer also supplies discount stores. They said supermarkets can be such dominant buyers for some manufacturers that they can extract ever-lower prices. The manufacturer has no alternative but to agree to the demands. The big five chains – Sainsbury's, Tesco, Safeway, Asda and Somerfield – control more than 75% of the UK grocery market and the number of superstores has increased from 457 in 1986 to 1,102 by the end of 1997. They vigorously deny acting against consumers' interests.

The CB Hillier Parker report states that out-of-town or edge-of-town superstores, which also sold non-food goods and services, caused problems for other town centre retailers such as post offices, pharmacies, and dry cleaners. In response the British Retail Consortium claimed it was simplistic to blame superstores for town centre problems. Mark Bradshaw, the consortium's director of planning, said "There are a whole lot of other reasons such as the levels of rents, rates and crime, together with traffic access. On a positive note, we are encouraged that Richard Caborn has identified two problems that need addressing; the fact that about half of all local councils still have not drawn up local plans and that local authorities must help identify and assemble development sites in town centres. You can have a large number of different owners on a particular site and there can easily be a 10-year delay before you are even allowed to start building." There is credence to be leant to both sides of the argument. There is, however, no doubting the massive impact made on the British landscape by the explosion in superstore developments over the last two decades. This *guide* aims to identify the major commentaries on this late 20th century phenomenon.

In the interim period since Kirby's work, a useful reference work appeared which helps guide the student towards the most relevant works in the field. Produced by Search Publications, *Retailing: an Information Sourcebook*[3] appeared in 1995 and offers a resumé of the different types of material available on the subject of retailing. In some ways it serves as a link between *Shopping in the Eighties* and this present guide. The Sourcebook has useful sections on the distributive trades, employment in retailing, shopping patterns and the retail/consumer interface, and property, planning and retail location. As a starting point, the Sourcebook provides a good general overview of the literature of retailing in its broadest sense. Details of the main trade journals and the relevant trade bodies are provided. Of particular value is the bibliographic listing of textbook material and the helpful guide to key library collections and directory listings. The aim of this *guide* is to continue the work of Kirby and the Sourcebook in providing an illustration of the currently available literature on the subject of retailing. Most of the works cited in this review of the literature are held in the collections of the British Library.

References

1   Kirby D, *Shopping in the Eighties* – London: British Library, 1988.

2   Superstores sap the High Street, *The Guardian*, 26/9/98.

3   *Retailing: an Information Sourcebook* – Glasgow: Search Publications & Consultancy Services, 1995.

1. Can the High Street survive?

In 1995 Rob Harris sparked a discussion on the state of the nation's high streets. Analysing the results of research conducted by Gerald Eve he states "High streets are under threat: the evidence is all too apparent. But are they doomed?"[1] Gerald Eve had asked this question of over 50 leading figures in the retail, financial services, property and investment industries, as well as town centre managers and senior planners from urban councils. Some were more pessimistic than others, but it is clear that life can return to the high street if the real estate industry, and every private and public sector organisation with a vested interest, work together.

It is apparent that many town centre problems are a management rather than a social issue. The economic power of out-of-town retailing lies not only with the efficient layout, controlled environment, plentiful and free parking, but also in its management structure. So whatever the initiatives needed to tackle the high street it is clear that the role of management is paramount: we have to find a way of managing town centres as businesses.

In principle, the key players in managing town centres (landlords, investors, retailers, businesses and local authorities) consider initiatives to revitalise town centres to be ideologically sound. However, when it comes to management and funding, inertia pervades and the "not invented here" and "it's not my problem" mentality persists. Unless this changes, and unless the town centre manager has real authority and the respect of all those concerned, any initiative will be bound to fail.

The report by Harris summarises the key actions for necessary players in the coming decade as follows:

Retailers and retail service businesses that occupy our high streets

- consider strategies for addressing the static retail spend
- work with local authorities to a common purpose
- ensure that property strategy is reviewed at board level
- utilise your existing property better

Property developers and investors

- recognise that occupiers are more demanding and improve services
- develop a flexible approach to lease structures
- rethink the role of the high street and consider new forms of investment
- overcome fragmented ownership with innovative approaches to partnership
- consider mixed use developments
- overcome entrenched attitudes to management
- take the lead role in management initiatives

Local authorities

- decide your high street is a winner
- exploit your high street's natural resources
- seek to provide diversity (not just shops)
- do not fight the car, plan for it
- encourage residential and employment opportunities
- promote 'civic pride'
- seek flexibility in applying the building regulations

Town centre managers

- organise appropriate funding
- carry out market and consumer research
- understand the history of your high street
- explore the opportunities
- make better use of what exists
- prepare a realistic business plan
- address access and transport issues through management initiatives
- implement small scale as well as large scale projects
- adopt lessons from corporate marketing practice
- compete head on with regional shopping centres.

Given that every high street or town centre is different, there is no blueprint to ensure success. Initiatives that work in one town centre may not translate elsewhere but some town centres *are* getting it right. Experience suggests that small, incremental initiatives will often have a greater positive impact than reliance on a single large project. Each high street will need to assess its resources, its threats, and its opportunities to effect positive change before evolving a startegy to secure its long term future.

Gerald Eve believes it is a myth that town centres are dying. High streets are clearly under threat: the evidence is all too clear. But will they wither and die? Not if the real estate industry, and those in the private and public sector with a vested interest, work together to stop the rot. *Whither the high street?* explores the issues facing the real estate industry and considers what is needed to secure the 'vitality and viability' which the Government and others with interests in town centres seek.

With something like 80% of the population living in an urban environment the role of the high street as the focus of communities is not in question. Despite out-of-town retailing, electronic shopping and other trends highlighted in Gerald Eve's study, the high street retains an important role in the lives of most people. The real challenge lies in shaping the future form and environment of the high street. Critical to this is the recognition that different high streets perform different functions for different groups of people. Some high streets will fare better than others and, indeed, some will wither. The property industry must seek to work with retailers, planners and the many others with vested interests to ensure that high streets do not contribute, or succumb, to some of the more disturbing aspects of social change.

Harold Couch has taken issue with the widely accepted view that town centres are in decline.[2] In a recent article in *Estates Gazette* Couch discusses the strengths and weaknesses of town centres, and considers whether they are clearly worse than they were 20 or 30 years ago. The process of improving quality, he says, has been given impetus by the British Council of Shopping Centres' Town Centre Environmental Award. The BCSC Award for New Shopping Centres has also raised standards and, with a few exceptions, the shopping centres of the 1980s and 1990s have, according to Couch, led to an improvement rather than a decline in the towns concerned. Outstanding examples cited include Bromley, Carlisle, Chester, Hanley, Kingston, Peterborough and Wakefield. These centres may in some cases have caused changes to the fringes of the towns concerned, but Couch feels confident that surveys would show that the majority of the shopping public would regard the facilities in these towns to be an improvement on those that existed, say, 20 years ago and in most cases the towns concerned would not have been better if no new centre had been developed.

What is needed is a more analytical approach to the assessment of the strengths and weaknesses of town centres as a basis for looking at ways in which further improvements can be achieved. Recent versions of government Policy Planning Guidelines 6 list criteria for assessing the 'vitality' and 'viability' of town centres and, provided satisfactory means of measuring these criteria can be devised, there should be a much more reliable basis for assessment. Couch admits that there are problems in some of our smaller country towns and in industrial areas where often there is a high level of unemployment. He concludes that we should make a much more objective assessment of the strengths and weaknesses of our town centres. He believes far more town centres have improved than declined, but there is still a need to initiate clearer and more reliable ways of assessing the criteria for vitality and viability. There should be guidelines for good practice, based on the many excellent examples throughout the country. Town centre management is now recognised as an important ingredient in the process and the establishment of the Town Centre Managers Association is a valuable contribution in this respect. Finally, there is a need to develop a policy for dealing with the car. Restricting out-of-town retail development will do little or nothing in this respect and, in Couch's view, the greatest threat to our town centres is the car itself.

The journal *Environment and Planning, Series A*, devotes most of its January 1998 issue to the continuing debate on contemporary retail development. Wrigley, writing the guest editorial, says that British towns and cities, so profoundly impacted by the building of out-of-town superstores in the 1980s and, more selectively, by the wave of regional shopping centres – Metro Centre, Merry Hill, Meadowhall, Lakeside – face new challenges and opportunities in the late 1990s. As he says, "On the one hand, revised and tightened land-use planning regulation, which has prioritised the viability and vitality of town centres, provides a mandate for reinvestment in central area retail development and the promise of a new era in which town centre management schemes and sympathetically coordinated transport policies create a positive climate for that reinvestment. But, on the other hand, a new wave of regional centres – Dumplington, White Rose, Cribbs Causeway, Blue Water – granted planning permission, and in the development pipeline before the regulatory tightening, is poised to break, with potentially massive effect." It is these issues, which lie at the interface of property market dynamics, corporate finance, operational strategies of firms, and the urban built form, that represent one of the major challenges for society in the years ahead.

Wrigley also contributes a major paper in this issue of *Environment and Planning, Series A*, contrasting the conflicting operations of the UK food store development process in the late 1990s[3]. In particular, an attempt is made to unpack critical dimensions of the debate which surrounds the Department of the Environment's Planning Policy Guidance Notes 6 and 13 and the so-called 'Gummer effect', which is seen as having actively discouraged green-field out-of-town development and provided a mandate for reinvestment in town centre retail development. By exploring new evidence on the changing economics of superstore development, the impact of tightened land-use planning regulation, and shifting patterns of capital investment, Wrigley offers a conceptual framework in which to understand a radically transformed retail development picture.

During the era of the so-called 'store wars' in the late 1980s and early 1990s, the major UK food retailers became locked into strategies of accumulation in which capital investment in new store expansion programmes became the all-consuming engine of corporate growth. In turn, British cities were transformed by the construction of more than 15 million ft^2 of new food retail selling space – equivalent to adding 14 city centre retail areas the size of Bristol – during an intense crescendo to one of the UK's more significant civil engineering programmes. Suddenly and dramatically that era came to an end. During a period of deep crisis in the industry, particularly during 1993-94, the major food retailers were engulfed by problems of property overvaluation, nonrecoverable initial investment, depreciation, the treatment of capitalized interest, alternative versus existing use valuation, and the wider implications of sunk costs for corporate strategy. Wrigley wonders how we are to develop an appropriate conceptual framework for understanding the postcrisis, mature market, phase of the retail sector in the UK in the late 1990s. He asks, "What are we to make of the radically transformed store development picture of the late 1990s?"

According to Wrigley, there are essentially two contrasting views about this issue. Urban planners read into the significantly altered superstore development process after 1993-94 a derailment of the out-of-town 'gravy train' by newly tightened land-use planning regulation, in particular the 1993 and 1996 revised versions of the Department of the Environment's Planning Policy Guidance (PPG) Note 6 *Town Centres and Retail Development*, together with PPG Note 13 *Transport*. Steered by Secretary of State for the Environment, John Gummer, the Conservative Government is seen in this view as having undergone an important philosophical shift, away from the Thatcher-Ridley free-market era of wholesale deregulation in land-use planning which had characterized the mid-1980s to late 1980s and towards a more environmentally sensitive agenda. That agenda, coincident with broader EU environmental policy pressures, tempered a continued commitment to 'competition and choice' in the retail system with a desire to protect and enhance the 'vitality and viability' of existing town centres. Reinforced by symbolic planning appeal decisions – for example, rejection of the applications for a regional shopping centre at Duxford near Cambridge and superstores impacting historical centres such as Bath and Ludlow – and by the sequential approach to new retail development incorporated in the 1996 PPG6 following a recommendation in the House of Commons Environment's Committee's report *Shopping Centres and their Future*, the so-called 'Gummer effect' is seen as having actively discouraged green-field out-of-town development and provided a mandate for reinvestment in town centre retail development.

In contrast, more cynical retail analysts, whilst acknowledging that PPG6 and PPG13 have significantly increased the difficulty of development, ask to what extent tightened planning regulation has served merely to strengthen trends born out of the traumas of the 1993-94 crisis. In this view, dramatically changing and much harsher conditions of competition, plus acceptance by the major food retailers of the need to correct the overvaluation of their property portfolios, left these firms wary, highly cautious about committing similar mistakes to those which had accompanied the headlong rush to develop the large out-of-town superstores of the late 1980s and early 1990s – in particular, the payment of significant premiums for superstore sites, on the basis that they were to be used for profitable food retailing, well in excess of any conceivable alternative use value which might be realized on exit from those sites. Whilst discounting the attempt to gain tactical competitive advantage implicit in, Chairman of Asda, Archie Norman's well-known statement that PPG6 is "the best thing that has happened to the food industry", these analysts take the view that Norman's statement contains an important element of truth. The major food retailers have learned by bitter experience the lessons of over-commitment to what increasingly amounted to a single dominant strategy of capital accumulation – growth via 'conforming' out-of-town new store development. Instead, they have been forced to seek new ways to gain profitable market share – by exploring new types of store development, by reconsidering old locations of profit extraction, by more actively pursuing market extension acquisitions, by expanding new product areas within their mix and targeting the trade of weaker sectors of high street retailing, by developing consumer loyalty programmes and linking those programmes to the retailing of financial services, by redeploying more of their capital investment into sectoral diversification and internationalization, and so on. In this view, some of the retreat from out-of-town green-field superstore development commonly ascribed to PPG6 and the Gummer effect would have occurred in any event and has been misattributed. Indeed, the more restrictive climate of planning regulation is often regarded in this view as a 'blessing in disguise' for the major retailers allowing them "to ascribe their reductions in superstore development to the hostile planning situation instead of exposing them to accusation of decreasing profitability of new stores."

Wrigley goes on to argue that the PPG6 effect is real but should not be overexaggerated. As evidence on the changing economies of new store development in the post-property-crisis period has gradually begun to emerge, so has evidence on the impact of tightened land-use planning regulation. After an era in which land-use planning regulation regarding superstore development had been relatively lenient and in which planning application refusals by local authorities were often overturned on appeal to the Secretaries of State, figures for the period 1993-1997 show that suddenly appeals against the refusal of planning permission involving 64 superstores and an estimated 1.9 million ft^2 of sales area were rejected. The appeal refusal rate of 68% during this period is significantly higher than during the period of the 'store wars' in the late 1980s and early 1990s when annual appeal-refusal rates of under 50% were the norm and a smaller percentage of superstore applications went to appeal.

Moreover, tightened land-use planning regulation under the revised PPG6 and PPG13 appears to have triggered a qualitative shift in an important aspect of the superstore planning application process. The 'gentleman's agreement' which largely operated during the 'store wars' era, under which the major food retailers did not make objections to each others' planning applications, appears to have broken down. Intervention in rival operators' planning applications and planning appeals has become increasingly common, with the aim of avoiding loss of market share by preventing or, at the very least, stalling a rival's store development. In addition, the food retailers have increasingly challenged their rival's planning consents via judicial review or via the High Court.

As Table 1.1 below demonstrates, contrary to the impression sometimes given, the new store development programmes of the major food retailers have certainly not become 'defunct'. They continue to roll out and transform the built environment of the United Kingdom – albeit at a somewhat reduced level and with a mix that involves new stores that on average are somewhat smaller and are significantly less expensive to build. Indeed, the chairmen of both leading food retailers, whilst stressing the difficulties of "negotiating planning permissions for suitable sites with local authorities who want to stop food shopping taking place outside their local communities" in the context of the revised PPG6, note how they have "adjusted site search to the new realities", "adapted to the Government's changes in planning policy", and are now "obtaining planning permissions for new stores at a satisfactory rate" resulting in a "recovering supermarket opening programme" (Sir Ian MacLaurin, Tesco, and David Sainsbury, Company Annual Reports 1995/1996).

Table 1.1 Total numbers of new stores opened by major UK food retailers, 1992-1997

	1992–93	1993–94	1994–95	1995–96	1996–97
'Big 4' new stores	77	72	70	52	61

It is clear that the reduced build costs of new stores allied to physical distribution, logistics and systems developments, and the need to pursue market share in an environment of tightened land-use planning regulation have resulted in an important reconsideration of locations which during the height of the 'store wars' era were regarded as having catchments too small for profitable new store development. For example, by the end of 1996-97 Tesco had built more than 50 'compact' format new stores of between 16,000-26,000 ft^2. Often these were in smaller towns that had previously remained beyond the reach of the superstore-building programme. Increasingly, these 'compact' and country town stores are adjacent ('bolted-on') to the high street and are far less modular in design than the new stores of the late 1980s and early 1990s.

Wrigley believes the superstore-building age of the late 1980s and early 1990s will long be remembered for its profound impact on Britain's built form and cultural landscape and is deeply rooted in the nation's collective memory. As *The Times* columnist Simon Jenkins wryly commented at the height of the 1997 General Election campaign: "Eras are rarely remembered for what most obsessed politicians at the time. Victorian Britain was convulsed over Catholic emancipation and Home Rule but we think of it as nation of railways and Empire ... The Tory years will be recalled not for trade union reform or privatisation but for how a rural landscape was bespattered with housing estates and shopping centres. The cathedrals of Mrs Thatcher's Britain will be St-Tesco's-on-the-Roundabout and St-Sainsbury's-on-the-Interchange".[4]

Wrigley argues that it is difficult to say what would have happened to store development programmes in the mid to late 1990s had land-use planning regulation not been tightened. He does feel, though, "that the pain of confronting the problems of property overvaluation, the need to reevaluate overcommitment to a corporate strategy which had served the major food retailers well in the 1980s and early 1990s but which was gradually producing less satisfactory returns, and the changing economics of new store development, have been influences moulding the retail development picture of the mid to late 1990s which are as real as the impacts of PPG6 and PPG13."

In the same issue of *Environment and Planning, Series A*, Guy examines the recent surge in development interest and land values associated with retail park development in the United Kingdom.[5] This surge is shown to have arisen from changes in retailing methods among leading nonfood retailers and in land-use planning regulations which have created concerns over scarcity of land for future off-centre development. The implications for both set-up and exit sunk costs for retailers, and alternative-use values for their land holdings, are discussed. Guy also suggests that off-centre retailing may be subject to rapid changes in the next few years as the potential for maximisation of value from existing retail parks is sought by developers and financial institutions. In another article, Guy discusses the extent to which land-use planning policies, intended to restrict growth in non-food retail development, have been successful. He shows that the main method of restricting off-centre schemes to acceptable occupiers lies in the imposition of planning conditions. Case study work in south Wales shows that this form of control has been ineffective when overruled by more liberal policies of central government.

Guy attempts to extend some of the recent critical discussion of retail planning policy away from the well-worn themes of grocery store development and regional shopping centres to other sectors of retailing. He shows that "land use planning policy in the UK has been an important influence on the pace and nature of off-centre retail development. Initially, a very cautious approach, protective of town centres, restricted off-centre non-food retailing to sales of DIY and other 'bulky' goods. In the early 1980s, many local authorities began routinely to allow sales of electrical goods from off-centre locations: in retrospect, this change in policy, which was hardly discussed at all in the practice literature at the time, was crucial. It raised the level of trading density obtainable from retail warehouses, thus encouraging growth in rent demands and capital values. It also set a precedent for allowing 'high street' retailing in off-centre locations."[6]

Guy provides a useful potted history of the planning policies adopted in the late 1980s and early 1990s. He feels that the central government policies introduced from 1993 onwards aimed at restricting further off-centre development arrived too late, especially where considerable off-centre development had already occurred. Guy believes "there are still steps that local authorities can take to protect their town centres from off-centre competition. Policies which attempt to enhance town centres and place firm criteria to limit off-centre development will be supported by Secretaries of State...One other matter which may help local authorities in future years concerns the status of time-expired planning consents for off-centre development. In response to the House of Commons Select Committee, the Department of the Environment, Transport and the Regions has confirmed that where existing retail development permissions granted under the previous PPG 6 provisions have lapsed, any application for renewal of permission should be considered afresh, using the sequential approach set out in the present PPG6... However, it still appears that competitive pressure upon many town centres will become more severe in the short term as the property market acts according to its own interests. Local authorities will need more than ever to take positive steps to make their town centres more attractive and convenient for all types of shopping."[7]

The final paper in the special *Environment and Planning, Series A*, feature on retail development is a contribution by Langston, Clarke and Clarke on the subject of retail saturation.[8] In a paper that appeared in 1997, Langston, Clarke and Clarke had presented a picture of the provision of British food retail floor-space which was attentive to both the debate on retail saturation and the underlying competitive processes shaping the geography of the grocery sector.[9] They argued that there was still considerable variation in the provision of food retailing floor-space in the United Kingdom, with analyses presented at the regional, interurban and intraurban levels. It was concluded that saturation can only ever be a local phenomenon and that there was still considerable potential for retail expansion. They also suggested that such expansion was unlikely to occur without a notable degree of change in the complexion of the sector. In their 1998 paper, Langston, Clarke and Clarke update this analysis and present arguments pertaining to food retail change during the middle of this decade, i.e. following the property crisis that halted the earlier 'golden age' of store expansion, by focusing on recent change in terms of both retail fascia and locality.

Langston, Clarke and Clarke cite the three main reasons behind the ending of the 'golden age' of British food retailing during 1993-94 as follows. Firstly, the dominant food retailers suffered the effects of a major property crisis, causing them to adopt policies of asset depreciation and to write off the capitalised interest on the finance used to fund the superstore development programmes of the 1980s. Secondly, there have been changes in planning legislation, which have effectively turned against out-of-town developments in favour of town and city centre investments. The revised PPG6 legislation has to a considerable extent halted new out-of-town, green-field, developments, thereby overturning years of laissez-faire government policy regarding retail development. Finally, and perhaps most controversially, many commentators have suggested that the slowing down of large-scale developments was simply inevitable, given the fact that suitable sites were becoming increasingly hard to find. Though ultimately inseparable from the first two issues, this last point raises explicitly the question of market saturation. The authors proceed to discuss the idea of saturation within the context of the food retail market of the mid-1990s.

In contrast to the talk of market saturation, supermarkets recently received a boost as new research suggested that Britain needs more of them.[10] A report by GMAP, the retailing consultant, says that contrary to popular belief, the large supermarket groups are nowhere near to saturating Britain. While Hereford, Cheshire and Tayside rank as Britain's 'most saturated' areas, other places, including Inner London, Cambridge and South Yorks, have plenty of room for new stores. Strict rules on building out-of-town mean that Tesco, Sainsbury's, Safeway and Asda, the big supermarket groups, will have to concentrate on building smaller stores in high streets and in rural areas, says Professor Martin Clarke, author of the research. He also points out that none of the big four groups is yet truly national in scope, and that local battles are likely as each seeks to acquire the remaining regional brands. Meanwhile, the Fabian Society has called for the Government to have a rethink on retailing. It says that out-of-town planning rules should be liberalised and 'reviewed to balance consumer and employment interests with environmental concerns.'

In recent years some of the most famous names to be found on the high street have been put up for sale. Among the more prominent have been the 135-strong Littlewoods stores chain and Sears' British Shoe Corporation. This has lead to a flood of property on to the market – on top of the thousands of bank and building society branches that have become available through closures over the past few years – threatening to stall the recent revival of the high street, which has been boosted by the tightening of planning permission for out-of-town centres. Some industry observers fear that with supply out-stripping demand, boarded-up shop fronts will soon be seen in high streets throughout the country. Or alternatively, a further rash of charity shops – one of the few growth areas on our beleagured streets.

Others, however, are less pessimistic. The demise of the Littlewoods name, which made its high street debut in 1937, and the destruction of BSC are, they say, an inevitable result of the major structural changes that have been reshaping Britain's town centres in recent decades. Their place will simply be taken not only by the new breed of up and coming retailers but increasingly by theme pubs, restaurant chains and leisure-oriented retailers.

A prime example of the changing face of the high street can be seen in Kingston, already one of the country's top 20 shopping centres, according to Robin Bevan, director of retail consultancy Management Horizons Europe. He says: "Kingston has attracted a number of emerging retail formats and the opening of the Bentall Centre has helped accelerate changes that are happening at perhaps a slightly slower rate all over the country. It gives us a number of clues about the British high street of the next five years." The Kingston experience reveals a number of trends, notably the growing leisure-based element of the high street, from theme restaurants to music, computer and video game specialists. While there were 250 shops in Kingston 10 years ago, there are now 311. The multiples are increasingly dominant and now account for almost two thirds of retail stores, against fewer than half 10 years ago. There is also a growing international flavour, with the proportion of international retailers in the centre rising from less than 3% 10 years ago to 9%, including Gap, Disney, Morgan and Talbots.

Leisure-orientated retailers are among the clear winners of the past 10 years, with significant growth in computer games outlets, sportswear, travel agents and music. Mobile phone shops have also mushroomed, while in music, chains such as HMV and Virgin have been winning a bigger market. All this has been at the expense of more traditional retailers such as shoe sellers, jewellery shops, pharmacies, hardware stores and TV rental shops. Retail analysts Corporate Intelligence say competition between the leisure and retail sector will continue, with spending on leisure outstripping that on retailing. One clear trend has been the boom in theme restaurants. The number, including pizza and pasta chains, has tripled to more than 3,400 in the past 10 years.

Competition for the best sites is fierce and Whitbread has snapped up a number of former clearing bank branches for its Café Rouge and Dôme chains. With spending on eating out forecast by the Henley Centre to soar from £21.4 billion to £32 billion over the next four years, the restaurants boom shows no sign of abating. Meanwhile, the winners among retailers will be those who offer what the marketing world calls "a total shopping experience." Nineties shoppers don't just want to buy, they demand to be entertained as well. Moving in the right direction are fashion chains such as Next, which now has restaurants in 17 of its branches. Bookshops, too, are starting to instal coffee shops to encourage customers to browse.

Along with the seemingly unstoppable rise of the theme restaurant, high streets of the future will see more stores with an educational or fun bias. Also on the up will be manufacturer brand stores such as Levi's and Nike. Corporate Intelligence's Robert Clark says: "As demand for more pleasurable shopping grows, so the forces to combine retail and leisure will increase. Centres with an appropriate mix of leisure will attract higher footfall, more spending – and stronger retail demand."

A wave of out-of-town developments, from multiplex cinemas to business parks, is steadily undermining the tougher planning controls introduced by the Government in 1996, according to countryside groups. While conceding that the new guidelines had forced the big stores to think again, they warned that councils were ignoring the Government by pushing through other projects on green field sites. As a report warned that curbs were needed to halt the spread of business parks, planning minister Robert Jones conceded that some councils were ignoring environmental considerations. He spoke out after the report, from the UK Round Table on Sustainable Development, had said that a road building programme to serve out-of-town developments would lead to a traffic pollution time bomb.

Tough planning guidelines, introduced in 1994 and strengthened in 1996, have led to a sharp decline in planning applications for shopping centres. Figures produced by consultants and chartered surveyors Hillier Parker show that large shopping projects in the pipeline and under construction have dropped from a peak of 8.72 million square metres in 1988 to 2.64 million in 1996. But Chris Goddard, a partner with Hillier specialising in retailing, said more people were being attracted to revamp centres. He said customer demand for other projects, such as multiplex cinemas, meant that developers could often only find sufficiently large sites out of town.

The largest out-of-town shopping centre in Britain is the Metro Centre on the edge of Gateshead, which attracts 100,000 visitors on a typical Saturday. Whether the mammoth £400 million complex, with 340 shops and 5,000 workers, would get planning permission today under the new out-of-town guidelines is open to question. The Council for the Protection of Rural England (CPRE) pointed out that further green field development could only push up car use. The Round Table report said the Government had not done the detailed work necessary to follow through its existing planning curbs. The CPRE said that while the Government was pursuing this welcome policy, the real cost of driving a car was going down and the cost of using public transport was rising. The report highlights Northampton, where Barclaycard is building a new out-of-town headquarters and plans to move in 2,500 workers from other areas, saving more than £1 million a year in running costs. Robert Jones blamed local councils for the mess. "With 400 planning authorities, trying to get the message across to all of them at the same time is difficult. There are a lot of council leaders who think they would rather have jobs than have the sort of environmental quality we think is right."

A report from URBED, the Urban and Economic Development Group, sponsored by some of the major retailers and property investors in the UK, along with the Department of the Environment, sets out the challenges for town centres and comments on good practice.[11] Interest in sustaining and improving town centres has been growing over several years. Town centre managers are well established in over 150 places. Central government planning policy issued in 1996 says that town centres, rather than out-of-town sites, should be the preferred location for retail development. The new Labour government has endorsed this approach and says that it is strongly committed to ensuring that existing town, city and district centres act as the focus for investment, so as to provide easy access to a wide range of facilities and services by public transport as well as private cars.

However, many town centres find it difficult to compete with out-of-town developments. All of the interests – commercial and public sector – need to pull together to ensure that centres are vital and viable for the future. British towns are different from most of the rest of Europe in their dependence on ad hoc co-operation: businesses are not so involved in local affairs, and membership of Chambers of Commerce is not compulsory. The potential for improvement is considerable, but, as URBED says, the management, organisation and resourcing of town centre management initiatives do not yet measure up to the tasks. The researchers found over 200 initiatives, but of very variable character. Some are limited to liaison meetings, and less than half have a distinct budget. URBED reports on several surveys, and 47 case studies of good practice.

The first of three main sections explains how to launch an initiative, the need to bring together all those with the powers and resources to affect a town centre, the need to develop a shared vision and clear strategy, the likely priorities; the need for funding arrangements, for proper organisation and for monitoring results. Next is a section discussing alternative models of partnership between the public and private sectors, the ways partnerships develop, and, looking at the precedents established by Bristol and Coventry, the benefits of setting up a Town Trust. This is a corporate organisation to provide services in town centres. The following section discusses how and why to monitor performance, in things like property values, footfall, and business attitudes. There is a crucial need to demonstrate benefits, in order to acquire and maintain funds from the partners.

Funding is the key long term question. Significant changes in town centres need significant investments. The final section of URBED's report is far more controversial than the rest. It considers who should pay for improvements in town centres, from pedestrianisation to public transport. Current initiatives are reliant on a 'begging bowl' approach to commercial companies, and what the authors say is an over-reliance on bidding for public funds which creates a 'lottery' and discourages proper planning and budgeting. It is suggested that North American Business Improvement Districts provide a possible model, where if an initial ballot in a town approves a scheme, it becomes mandatory on business to contribute for a set period of time. The Investment Priority Areas of Ireland suggest another model. Finally they state that the existing business rating system (local property tax) needs urgent reassessment: local councils have little control over their resources in reality; there is no incentive to prioritise their spending on town centres; the tax appears to bear more heavily on small than large business; in contrast, the system works against the larger towns as a whole; occupiers not owners are charged the rates so that those who arguably have most at stake in towns have little direct contribution. All these points are controversial, and made even more so by the huge political problems experienced in the UK the last time the system was overhauled.

Town Centre Partnerships is important at two levels. Firstly, it is a practical and encouraging guide to those involved at local levels in the businesses of town centres, in Britain but elsewhere too. Secondly, its final chapter indicates what difficult reforms must be contemplated by central government, if British towns are to be better managed.

One of the most important works to consider the future of retailing from a socio-economic viewpoint was produced by the Institute for Public Policy Research in 1995. The paper, produced by Raven and Lang, studied a range of concerns over retail concentration and the rise of the supermarket giants.[12] They contrast the reputation of supermarkets as paragons of the free market with the reality of market failure. Through their reliance on car-travel amongst their consumers, long-haul road freight, industrialised farming and the excessive use of packaging, supermarkets give rise to social costs which they do not bear themselves; in that sense they are heavily subsidised – at the cost of the environment and disadvantaged social groups. These costs are not internalised in the price of food. The benefits for some consumers – convenience, choice, and low prices – are at the expense of others without access to supermarkets – typically the old, the car-less and the poor. There are winners, but there are also losers.

Past reviews of the food retail sector by the Office of Fair Trading and the Monopolies and Mergers Commission have concluded that there is, as yet, no infringement of UK competition law. This paper suggests that the point above which the dangers of monopoly are conventionally held to apply – 25% of any given market – is not appropriate for food. It argues that food shopping is at a local level. Meanwhile the focus of competition policy is moving in the opposite direction – to the even more remote European market. This tendancy is a cause for concern.

Raven & Lang's paper argues that public debate about the social, environmental and economic consequences of rising retail concentration is an urgent priority. It makes a number of detailed recommendations – for competition policy, institutional change, planning regulations, transport policy, local enterprise, and packaging.

The paper draws heavily on the House of Commons Environment Select Committee report 'Shopping Centres and their Future'. The Government report was important in its call for restrictions on the building of supermarkets on out-of-town sites. The Committee found that "the task now at hand is to regenerate and sustain the nation's shopping heritage" through "reducing reliance on the car in the long term", and expressed concern about the need to give consumers "access to a wide range and choice of convenient and attractive shopping facilities selling goods at competitive prices." Serious questions were beginning to be asked.

Raven & Lang argue that supermarkets, long perceived as paragons of the free market, are in fact nothing of the sort. It is argued that "they do not fulfil the preconditions for the perfectly competitive market of economic textbooks, which presupposes many small firms, vying to outdo each other and entering and leaving the market as some prosper and others fail. Instead there are a few huge retailers, getting bigger all the time and furiously resisting new competitors. Classically, consumers should be able to make their purchases on the basis of full and fair information. Instead shoppers have become increasingly uneasy about the way food is produced, and have only confusing and inadequate labelling to guide them. Classically, the price of goods should reflect their true cost and not exclude significant social or environmental costs. Instead, the real costs of transport, excessive packaging and the intensive horticulture associated with supermarkets are simply not reflected in supermarket prices."[13]

The paper shows that supermarkets' policies skew resource allocation so that, in the shorter term, there are significant 'external' social and environmental costs which are borne by others. The authors acknowledge at the outset that much of the responsibility for market failure lies with public policy, which allows financial costs and social costs to diverge. In the cases of transport and packaging, for example, public policy is certainly at fault; but food retailers do not escape blame, since they account for a singularly high – and grossly disproportionate – share of the total external costs. In other areas, the market failures are specific to the sector. In both categories, things will not change without intervention – through correcting misleading price signals, in the form of an effective competition policy, and through support for alternative ways of getting food to the people, and the people to the food.

The impact of supermarkets on the transport sector, for instance, is threefold: they create increased demand for personal transport (particularly cars) amongst consumers; they increase demand for freight transport, by transporting goods further; and they use their considerable political influence in demanding upgraded transport infrastructure, particularly roads. Raven & Lang present figures which highlight the increase in car usage caused by the development of edge-of-town and out-of-town supermarket sites. Whilst stores may protest to the contrary, the costs in terms of pollution and congestion are considerable. Research has shown that while 62% of people used a car in 1985 for their main grocery shopping, by 1991 this was up to 66%, and by 1993 it was up again to 73%.

The large supermarkets are also criticised for being less than environmentally-friendly in their approach to food packaging. For instance, there has been strong resistance in the UK to the EC Directive Containers of Liquids for Human Consumption (1985) which recommends the use of refillable containers. The UK's very poor record in this area is overwhelmingly the responsibility of the supermarkets. A Government study of returnable containers found that "the stocking policy of supermarkets ... favours non-returnables and ... has largely contributed to non-returnables attaining their present share of the market." Evidently the supermarkets do not envisage a change of policy: they predict continuing growth in packaging waste. So long as much of the supermarkets' *modus operandi* depends upon long-haul freight, industrial production and extended shelf-life, large quantities of packaging will remain indispensable to them. Were they to be liable for the full costs of their decisions – in other words, were the market failures to be corrected – their distribution patterns would probably change radically, and their reliance upon packaging rapidly diminish.

Raven and Lang look at the serious damage inflicted on the UK horticultural industry by the increase in reliance of the major supermarkets on overseas produce. According to the trade journal *The Grower*, supermarkets are demanding products out of season "shopping anywhere in the world at world surplus prices." The ability to supply fresh seasonal foods from around the world has been one of the supermarkets' proudest boasts – with very prominent and expensive advertising campaigns like Safeway's extolling the virtues of green beans fresh from Mount Kilimanjaro. "The British fruit market is particularly vulnerable to invasion because buying is concentrated in supermarkets", which costs rural jobs, as large areas of land formerly growing labour-intensive, high-value horticultural crops revert to agriculture. Import penetration can be rapid and on a large scale: "Spanish shipments of iceberg lettuce to Britain are expected to rise ... this year to 79,000 tonnes. This compares with only 1,600 tonnes in 1985", causing British growers to dump large quantities of produce.

Supermarkets avoid dependance on natural growing seasons by encouraging protected cropping. In addition to being a major energy-consumer, glasshouse production uses a wide range of materials with significant environmental impacts. Large quantities of oil-based synthetic materials such as polyurethane, polystyrene, polythene, polyester and PVC are used, as is aluminium – even more energy-intensive. "The additives necessary for their production – antioxidants, catalysts, biocides and pigments – are most damaging to the environment, and indeed to plants. Different stages in the life-cycles of these materials pose different pollution risks, starting with the extraction of raw materials and ending with recycling and disposal." As Raven & Lang re-iterate, these external costs are not, of course, reflected in supermarkets' prices.

Off our Trolleys? provides useful background on the town and country planning issues at work in the retailing environment. Under the banner of 'reshaping the landscape', Raven & Lang confirm that "the financial muscle and expertise of supermarkets makes them formidable operators of the planning system".[14] Typical of the public statements of supermarkets on their site development policies is

Sainsbury's claim that even on greenfield sites, development will be considered "normally only when as a result of the development the overall public benefit in terms of open space or environmental terms is undiminished or preferably enhanced." Similarly, Tesco reassures that "concern that store development is having any material impact on greenfield locations is unfounded." This fits uneasily with the well-documented record of environmental damage caused by supermarket construction.

The claim by many supermarkets to, in Tesco's words, "support the well-being of the community" is disputed by some of the communities concerned. In Bristol, 16,664 local people objected in writing to a proposed Tesco store, backed by Bristol City Council, Avon County Council, the local MP and MEP, all the local political parties, the city's new Bishop and numerous local amenity groups. Tesco ignored the views of the community, built their supermarket and resorted to litigation to prevent demonstrations by local residents.

Raven and Lang lend weight to the suspicion that supermarkets have led the way in the run-down of the high street. According to the Automobile Association "out-of-town shopping centres ... for a mainly car-borne consumer market are a trend pioneered by food retailers such as Sainsbury." In 1988, for example, 65% of new superstores opened were edge- or out-of-town, with only 10% in town centres. In the year to spring 1992, 72% of Sainsbury's sales were from edge- or out-of-town sites; for Safeway the figure was 84%, and for Tesco 87%. Inevitably this diverts business away from – and thus undermines the viability and vitality of – existing shopping centres. Surprisingly, food retailers frequently deny that their developments have this effect. According to Tesco, "concern is sometimes expressed about the impact that out of town shopping facilities have on the traditional high street. All the evidence in recent years has shown that in fact the effect is beneficial." This view is contradicted by research commissioned by Tesco themselves – including that which concluded principally that "the health of the High Street has deteriorated in many larger towns and city centres ... (and) there is serious concern that the emergence of new, outlying shopping centres will compound this problem." Many of the supermarkets' own high street outlets have closed after they have opened edge- or out-of-town stores – corroborating the wealth of conclusive evidence that out-of-town retail development undermines the viability of established town-centre shopping facilities.

Moreover, a common practice of supermarkets when moving out-of-town is to prevent their former sites remaining in the grocery sector, by refusing to sub-let to potential competitors. Unless other retail space is available, this will often leave shopping centres with no significant grocery outlet – reducing the number of shoppers and threatening the viability of other local shops.

In cases where planning permission might be in doubt, supermarkets are able to offer 'planning gain', otherwise known as Section 106 agreements (after the relevant part of the Town and Country Planning Act 1990). These are sometimes worth several millions of pounds, and offer improvements to local facilities to 'buy off' local opposition in return for planning permission. While the applicants' intention may simply be public-spirited, it is at least arguable that it tends to weigh heavily in their favour and against the less organised interests of small independent shops which, needless to say, do not have the resources to offer this sort of largesse.

Any inclination by the authority to refuse planning permission will be tempered by the knowledge that, though such a decision may be in line with the authority's strategic plans, it would often be overturned on appeal by the Department of the Environment. In such circumstances the authority would risk liability for costs, and the supermarket's offer would be withdrawn. Faced with such a possibility, many local authorities have caved in and granted permissions against their better judgement.

In recognition of the damage to town centres caused by out-of-town development, the Government published new planning guidelines in March 1994. The Department of the Environment Planning Policy Guideline Note 13 (PPG13) was heralded in advance by the Environment Secretary John Gummer as "hailing the revival of the British High Street and the demise of the out-of-town shopping centre." Less partial commentators claim the Government's new policy will have a more modest effect. With respect to out-of-town retail development, the guidance note relies on policy guidelines from July 1993, but only two of the 132 paragraphs specifically covered retailing, and they suggested the July note gave definitive guidance. It did not, as was recognised by the House of Commons Environment Select Committee report *Shopping Centres and their Future* in November 1994.

In addition to the uncertainty about whether the changes in planning policy will make any difference, there is already enough out-of-town retail space with planning permission to accommodate the big three food retailers, at current rates of expansion, into the next century. Any reduction in store-opening programmes, according to the Institute of Grocery Distribution, the grocery retailers' research organisation, is in recognition of the changing economics of the market-place rather than a direct reaction to the current debate on planning.

Raven and Lang debate the social implications of the shift towards out-of-town retailing. They are concerned that the poorer classes no longer have access to the bargains associated with the larger supermarkets. A study by Malseed, *Bread without Dough: Understanding Food Poverty* (1990), examining a group of low and high income consumers, found that "all the Affluent Group did the bulk of their shopping at out-of-town multiples ... which they say are cheaper than the local shops ... None of the Affluent Group encounter access problems as they all possess cars, which they use for the bulk of their shopping." This reflects the strong correlation between distance travelled for shopping and social class. Since supermarkets are situated mainly at edge- or out-of-town sites, the convenience and price advantages of supermarket shopping are often out of reach of the poorest in society. They do not have cars and have difficulty in using increasingly expensive and unreliable public transport. It seems that only if you live next to the supermarket with the lowest prices could you benefit without having extra costs in transport.

Raven and Lang claim that supermarkets embody certain market failures. *Off Our Trolleys?* tries to show that "supermarkets may not give consumers the lowest prices; in effect they discriminate against the poorest in society; and they offer a choice of goods that depends on importing from a wide range of sources while in effect restricting the diversity of domestic production in any given area. Worse still, their use and disposal of packaging, impact on the transport and planning systems and on small farmers and growers show large and growing externalities, in the form of environmental damage. This is not reflected in the price of goods on supermarket shelves. Market theory predicts that if prices do not reflect true costs then the allocation of resources will be distorted; and so it has proved."[15]

In concluding, Raven and Lang make a number of recommendations under the headings of competition policy, town and country planning policy, transport, local enterprise and employment, and packaging. Their study includes a useful bibliography with 187 references.

Barclays Merchant Services, which handles the plastic card purchases made in more than 125,000 shops and business across the UK, have shown in a recent survey that high street retailers are finding it increasingly difficult to compete with out-of-town shopping centres. Three-quarters of the 1,000 small to medium-sized retailers questioned in the survey are worried about the decline of business on the high street as out-of-town shopping centres continue to grow in popularity and size. And more than two-thirds of them believe that out-of-town shopping centres have a negative effect on their business. Almost one in three retailers also think that urban life will never be the same again due to the growth of out-of-town shopping centres, while a quarter believe that they have an effect on conservation issues of local communities.

Tony Slater, sales and marketing director of Barclays Merchant Services, said: "Town centres have traditionally provided the cultural, social and commercial focus of daily life. However, as out-of-town shopping centres increase in popularity, many high street retailers have found it difficult to compete and our survey shows that they are concerned about their future. But as tougher planning regulations come into force and more investment is made to revitalise the high street, town centres and out-of-town developments will become complementary to each other." Smaller retailers are already experiencing some benefits to being based in or near to an out-of-town shopping centre. The survey found that more than half welcomed the ease of parking facilities for customers and an increase in the number of shoppers passing their store. Nearly 40% of retailers liked the convenient shopping atmosphere of out-of-town set-ups and almost a third preferred being located near to larger stores.

The period 1989-1996 witnessed a remarkable transformation in the UK government's policy concerning retail development and land use planning. This transformation has been marked by a spate of official publications, including three versions of a Planning Policy Guidance Note, three major commissioned studies and a Parliamentary Committee report. A review article by Guy considers all these publications, concentrating particularly on the commissioned studies by BDP Planning and OXIRM (1992), Roger Tym and Partners (1993) and URBED (1994).[16] Guy believes these are of interest and value beyond the more narrowly defined concerns of official policy.

For most of the 1980s, the Thatcher government displayed an attitude essentially of indifference towards the planning implications of retail development. This was part of a general approach in which statutory development plans were seen as barely relevant to the needs of the economy. In particular, plans were seen as being too conservative and too inflexible to be able to respond to development pressures from large property and retail firms. Much development (usually 'out-of-town') which had been considered undesirable by local planning authorities was thus allowed on appeal. Superstores, retail warehouse parks and regional shopping centres mushroomed at a time when continental European countries were imposing greater restrictions on off-centre development.

22

The first comprehensive statement of government policy emerged in the Planning Policy Guidance on 'major retail development' (Department of the Environment/Welsh Office,1988). This was one of a series of guidance notes which were gradually replacing central government circulars and development control policy notes.

Government policy in the form of PPGs interacts with the statutory land use planning system in two basic ways. First, it attempts to steer structure and local planning policies in directions which the government considers to coincide with the national interest, as defined of course in relation to party political objectives. Thus, a Conservative government which favours wealth creation and abhors local political intervention would naturally expect local authorities to allow every opportunity for private companies to develop further physical assets and profit-making centres. This first version of PPG6 had relatively little to say about the role of the development plan system in regulating retail growth. Locational choice was to be left to the private sector, and the land use planning system would simply react to proposals for development. It was emphasised that development plans were frequently out-of-date, and should be regarded as only one of a number of 'material considerations' in relation to any application for retail development.

The second function of PPGs is to prescribe the extent to which local planning authorities should control or modify proposals for development. Essentially the PPGs set up criteria which local authorities are expected to use in judging applications, and indicate to what extent refusals or planning conditions might be supported by central government in the event of appeals by developers. The 1988 version of PPG6 shows some recognition that the trading impact of new retail development is an important issue and one which might justify strategic control of retail development by local authorities. However, in a famous phrase first coined in 1985, the Note declares that "commercial competition as such is not a land use planning consideration": thus, the trading impact of a major new development is of relevance to planners only in "exceptional circumstances." These are where the effects "could seriously affect the vitality and viability of a town centre as a whole."

Guy states that the overall tone of the PPG was felt by commentators to be pro-development, especially of out-of-town retailing of food and 'bulky' goods, typified by superstores and retail warehouse parks. Practitioners also found some of the detailed guidelines to be ambiguous, provoking much argument at public enquiries.

During the early 1990s, events forced the government to reappraise its policy for retail development. First, under Secretary of State for the Environment Chris Patten, the development plan system was given greater comprehensiveness and status in the 1991 Planning and Compensation Act. This meant that the role of development plans in regulating retail development would have to be reconsidered. Second, the government showed first signs of 'greenness' through its promise, given at the Rio Conference of 1992, that carbon dioxide emissions would be restricted in future years. This implied greater control over out-of-town retail development, which was now seen as one of the causes of increased private car travel.

Events in the retail sector also caused concern. It became clear that some out-of-town development had caused severe trading impact upon existing town and district centres, leading to shop closures and a worsening physical environment. These trends were exacerbated by the effects of the economic recession, which affected consumer spending and itself led to many shop closures. Local authority associations and independent commentators had for many years been warning that out-of-town development would lead to town centre decline. However, it seemed that the government was unmoved by such arguments until it became obvious through the course of events that the situation had become serious.

Reacting to this increasing pressure for change, the DoE commissioned a 'literature review' on the 'effects of major out-of-town retail development' (BDP Planning and OXIRM, 1992). The authors of this study took a very broad view of this task: the literature examined covered not only out-of-town development and its impacts, but also retail change generally, the health of the 'high street', and the recent history of land use planning policy for retail development.

The report presents a classification of retail impacts which has become widely used in planning practice: economic, social and environmental. Each of these types of impact is defined and then illustrated from a very wide assembly of literature, much of which is itself criticised for lack of vigour. With a few exceptions, conclusions tend to be that actual examples of severe impact upon existing retail facilities are hard to find: the processes by which impacts are realised are tortuous and often obscured by other events, such as booms or slumps in consumer spending. Later sections review retail planning policy in local and central government, including the results of special surveys. The main value of the report lies in its clear exposition of trends in retail development in the UK, which itself helped develop a better understanding of these issues in government circles.

Following the warnings about the possible impacts of large-scale off-centre development, and the advice contained in the 1992 study, the Department of the Environment issued a draft revised version of PPG6. The final version (Department of the Environment/Welsh Office) contains radical revisions of policy. This guidance is dominated by discussion of 'town centres' rather than 'retail development.' It sets out means by which town centre 'vitality and viability' can be measured, and criteria by which off-centre proposals can be assessed for their effect on town centres. These criteria, however, still met with widespread criticism from town planning interests, principally because of the condition that, as previously, town centre vitality and viability 'as a whole' would have to be under threat for an off-centre proposal to be refused legitimately.

The revised PPG also gave much more prominence to the role of development plans in formulating retail planning policy and in the control of development. To some extent this merely reinforces the enhanced role of development plans introduced in the 1991 Planning and Compensation Act. However, development plans are also seen as a means of developing and reinforcing the role of town centres, and specific types of policy are set out. The guidance also defines conditions against which planning applications for large-scale regional shopping centres should be considered. While acknowledging that proposals for such centres could emerge from the structure planning process, the detailed conditions virtually rule out any likelihood of speculative applications for such centres being successful.

Two of the main emphases in the 1993 PPG6 are on the need for positive planning of town centres, and the importance of 'vitality and viability'; various methods of measuring these qualities are suggested. The Department of the Environment thus commissioned a further research study in order to clarify these issues and establish 'good practice' in town centre planning. The resulting report from URBED, as we have seen, contains a wide-ranging investigation of those qualities which characterise 'winners' and 'losers' amongst town centres. As Guy states, "these surveys reveal some worrying trends. Many town centres are at best stagnating: they offer neither an efficient environment for commercial interests, nor an attractive physical environment for the visitor."[17]

After a wide-ranging review of recent changes in the retail environment within and outside town centres, the study team discuss the 'responses' which local authorities and other agencies can put into effect. The two central chapters, on 'assessing vitality and viability' and 'devising town centre strategies', are likely to be those that are read the most attentively in planning offices. The study suggests 'four A's'

(Attraction, Accessibility, Amenity and Action) as elements of a 'healthy town centre'. They list over 30 different types of programme, under these four headings, which can be used to revitalise a town centre. The following chapter, which classifies town centres into five main types, introduces the discussion of 'good practice' which completes the report.

Concurrently with URBED's report, the House of Commons Environment Committee (1994) was investigating retail trends and retail planning policies. Through the conventional means of hearing evidence from interested parties, and paying visits to sites of interest, the committee was exposed to a wide spectrum of views. The Department of the Environment itself submitted a competent summary of recent trends and of its own retail planning policy, as expressed in PPG6 and the new PPG13 on Transport (Departments of the Environment and Transport, 1994).

The committee took a more protective line on town centres than the government had in PPG6. While not advising a complete ban on development outside town centres, the recommendation for a 'sequential approach' to the control of new development reflected a feeling that the out-of-town movement had already gone too far. The committee also called for more investment in public transport, and financial support for town centre management. These two last notions met with a lukewarm response from the Department of the Environment (1995a), which otherwise endorsed most of the committee's recommendations. The DoE commissioned a study into the impact of superstores on market towns and district centres, and made plans to commission a study on the cumulative impact of off-centre proposals on the vitality and viability of town centres.

In 1995 the Department produced draft revised guidance for planners (Department of the Environment, 1995b). This potential third version of PPG6, which was made available for consultation in July 1995, incorporates many of the House of Commons's Committee recommendations. It is worth noting the extent to which government policy for retail development has changed in the last 10 years. From a position which endorsed the wishes of developers and marginalised development planning, policy now emphasises the role of local authority development plans in regulating development; strongly supports town and district centres as first-choice locations for new retailing; and specifies stringent tests of acceptability for off-centre proposals. As Guy says, "a greater reversal in favour of established land use planning interests would be hard to imagine."[18]

According to Burke, the period 1995/96 was significant in that the year opened and closed with stories about the government's new approach to edge-of-town and out-of-town stores and shopping centres.[19] PPG6 is likely to have long lasting effects on competitive conditions, almost certainly in unintended and unanticipated ways. Only a hopeless cynic would note that just as financial commentators were concerned about edge-of-town saturation, the government limited scope for new entrants. The same cynic might also see a government backed return to the town centre as a blessed relief for recession hit property developers. However, as Burke says, since developers of out-of-town purpose-built shopping centres have yet to satisfy appetites, the cynic's speculations are probably out of order.

The justification for the change in planning policy – essentially a return to pre-1980's priorities – relates to concerns about the commercial health of town centres and to damage to the environment, which in many people's minds is associated with car and truck traffic. Road pricing, or some other form of traffic rationing, coupled with measures to regenerate town centres appear necessary for any voluntary shift in shopping patterns to occur. Location stands out as the competitive issue of the next few years. PPG6 will undoubtedly change the balance of competitive forces – the big question, according to Burke, is "in whose favour?"[20]

The Environment Select Committee's report on *Shopping Centres and their Future*[21] was welcomed by the Government, who tabled their own response in early 1995. They found the report represented a "valuable contribution to the current debate on the future of our town centres and the future location of retail development. The Government is firmly committed, as set out in PPG6, to sustaining and enhancing the vitality and viability of our town centres, to make these a major focus for investment, particularly retail development, and to facilitate competition from which all consumers can benefit."[22] Throughout the response the keywords are 'vitality' and viability'. This follows on from the DoE report of May 1994, *Vital and Viable Town Centres: Meeting the Challenge*.[23] In particular, it was felt that planning guidance "should include establishing the extent to which town centre and out-of-centre retailing can complement each other, without undermining the vitality and viabilty of existing centres".

The Government's response was structured as follows:

- revision of PPG6
- transport issues
- other guidance and changes in procedure

- good practice for town centre management
- financing town centre improvements
- research needs
- information needs.

The Government proposed to revise PPG6 in the light of comments made by the Select Committee. The Committee commented that "planning guidance has to be clear and consistent in order for retailers, local planning authorities and the development industry to operate efficiently and effectively. We believe that the sequential test advocated by Ministers – that a retail proposal should not be given planning permission outside a town or city if there is a suitable site within or close to the centre – provides an appropriate, clear first step in the adjudication of development proposals ... We recommend that planning policy guidance be amended to include a presumption that superstores are best located in or on the edge of town centres unless there are very strong indications to the contrary." The Government claimed that the sequential approach to looking for suitable sites was part of current policy. They did, however, accept that this approach should be applied by both developers and local planning authorities in seeking to identify suitable sites, and that it was particularly important for identifying sites through the development plan. The revision of PPG would encourage developers and local planning authorities to identify suitable sites through the development plan process. This, it states, may require more emphasis to be put in development plans on identifying suitable town centre and edge-of-centre sites for retailing. This would convey clearly to developers and retailers a positive and realistic approach to planning for retailing.

The Select Committee recommended that more detailed guidance be issued to local authorities as to the criteria and methods to be employed in carrying out impact studies for retail developments. In particular, they believed there to be "a need for better guidance on anticipated impacts – especially of the long-term social and environmental effects – in retail planning, so that these lessons can be used by local authorities as they finalise their development plans and in their assessment of planning applications." They recommended that the DoE commission more independent research into the impacts of retail developments, particularly into the "cumulative effects of out-of-town developments on the vitality and viability of existing centres." The Government agreed there was a greater need for awareness of the range of impacts of out-of-centre developments, not only trade diversion. Government planning policy guidance, especially PPG6, PPG12 and PPG13, emphasises the need for a broader assessment framework covering economic, social and environmental considerations. Such a framework, incorporating information on the impact on retailing, travel, access and on the environment, was needed to assess all major retail schemes.

The Committee expressed further concern over the product range of superstores and the transfer of pharmacies and post offices. Attention was drawn to the "adverse impact which large food stores can have on existing stores as their product range is broadened to include an extensive array of non-food goods. Pharmacies and post offices fulfil an important role in the community for all sections of the population, and their widespread distribution should be retained wherever possible." In response to this issue, the Government claimed to be concerned that out-of-centre stores "should not undermine the vitality and viability of town or local centres by removing key services which must continue to be accessible to all, such as pharmacies and post offices. This is especially important since many of those who depend on these services do not have the use of a car. Since licences for dispensing pharmacies are limited and usually can only be obtained by moving premises, the Government would be concerned by the loss of such services from existing centres."

Subsequent events, with the diversification of superstores into the retailing of pharmaceuticals and postal goods, have shown the Committee to be correct in voicing their concerns. The Council For The Protection Of Rural England, for example, has issued a warning that village shops are being wiped out by the spread of superstores, whose numbers have grown from 432 in 1986 to 1,034 in 1996. The Village Retail Services Association (ViRSA), formed five years ago as a result of a successful campaign to save a shop in Dorset, estimates that 3,500 village shops in Britain are in trouble, while a 1995 survey by the Rural Development Commission found that two-fifths of English rural parishes had no permanent shop. "Huge changes in the way we live and shop have resulted in local shops having to fight harder for their survival," says Gregor Hutcheon, CPRE rural affairs officer. "This is despite the fact that since the 1970s, 300 people a day have left urban areas to live in the countryside. Local shops bring vitality and diversity to villages and small communities."

One of the other key areas identified by the Committee is town centre management. They believe that the "indecision over how to fund town centre management initiatives has hindered the development of town centre management in Britain and must be resolved as a matter of urgency." They recommend that "the DoE work with local authorities, the Association of Town Centre Management and other relevant parties to examine existing evidence and evaluate which is the best way forward for promoting local accountabilty and for funding more effective partnerships between the public and private communities in town centres." The Government, in its response, pledged to promote public/private partnerships for improving and managing our town centres. The Department of the Environment aimed to help by disseminating good practice.

The Committee was also keen for the Government to consider funding town centre improvements from the Single Regeneration Budget. In response to this, the Government was able to point to the fact that town centre partnerships were eligible to bid for a share of the Single Regeneration Budget and that 40 schemes targeted on town centre revitalisation had been successful in the first round. Therefore over £350 million, about 20% of the finance available for 1995-96, had been allocated to town centre schemes. City Challenge, also part of the Single Regeneration Budget, funded 6 major town centre improvement schemes, with almost £36m committed over the five-year lifetime of each of the programmes. This was expected to lever in over £166m of private sector investment.

In the light of comments by the Committee, the Government commissioned a project to assess the impact of superstores on market towns and district centres. They also developed a further project on the impact of other types of out-of-town retail development, including the cumulative effects. This latter project, undertaken in 1995–96, included an assessment of retail warehouses, retail warehouse parks, warehouse clubs and factory outlets. Following a further recommendation, the Department of the Environment, in conjunction with the Department of Transport, proposed to look at travel patterns associated with different types of retailing as part of its follow-up work on PPG13. This research would prove useful in identifying key issues for policy action to improve access, car parking and public transport which can help promote more sustainable patterns of shopping, and to promote opportunities for combining trips for a number of purposes, so reducing the need for car travel.

Finally, the Committee welcomed the establishment of the Retail Statistics Working Group. The RSWG aimed to make the fullest use of existing sources of data and to limit new data collection to those areas not covered by exiting sources. The main information requirements to be identified were for data on floorspace, employment and turnover of retail outlets for town and other shopping centres.

As can be seen from the references listed at the end of this section, the early part of the decade saw a significant number of government sponsored publications aimed at heightening awareness of the problems engendered by the shift towards out-of-town retailing and the consequent diminution of the high street.[24-30] The phenomenon was not solely confined to England, as is illustrated by the references relating to a similar situation in Wales.

In Scotland, NPPG8 set out the Government's policy on retail development, including town centre development activities. It defines the factors that the Secretary of State has in mind when considering retailing policies and development proposals that come before him, and sets out the action required to be taken by planning authorities in their development plans and in development control. It revises and replaces the 1986 National Planning *Guideline on Location of Major Retail Developments*. This new guideline is of broader application in that it covers retail development and other related activities in town centres, as well as retail development in out-of-centre locations. It takes account of changes in retailing over the last ten years and emerging Government policy on sustainable development. The guidelines reiterate the sequential approach recommended by PPG6 in England and Wales. First preference should be for town centre sites, where suitable sites or buildings suitable for conversion are available, followed by edge-of-centre sites, and only then by out-of-centre sites in locations that are, or can be made, accessible by a choice of means of transport.

The guidelines contain a useful figure measuring vitality and viability, the bywords for Government policy on retail development in the 1990s:

"**Vitality** is a measure of how busy a centre is and **viability** is a measure of its capacity to attract ongoing investment, for maintenance, improvement and adaption to changing needs. Together, they can give an indication of the health of a town centre."[31] Various indicators can be used to provide an effective insight into the performance of a centre and so offer a framework for assessing vitality and viability, for example:

- *Pedestrian flow (footfall)* measures the numbers and movement of people on the streets. Counts should be collected on a consistent basis over a period of time, at different locations and times.
- *Prime rental values* provide a measure of the relative position of locations or streets within a centre and give an indication of retailer desire to locate within an area.

- *Space in use* for different town centre functions and how it has changed.
- *Retailer representation and intentions*; particularly by national multiples.
- *Commercial yield.* Generally, the lower the yield the more confidence that investors have in the long term profitability of the centre. Although a valuable indicator of retail viability, it needs to be used with care, as, in part, it reflect's a developer's, rather than a retailer's, interest in locating in an area.
- *Vacancy rates*, particularly street level vacancy in prime retail areas.
- *Physical structure of the centre*, including opportunities and constraints, and its accessibility.
- *Periodic surveys of consumers.*
- *Crime* – co-operation with the local police Architectural Liaison Service can assist in identifying persistent or potential problems in an area."

In 1994 the Scottish Office published a report, prepared by Professor John Dawson, analysing likely retail trends in Scotland during the rest of the 1990s. The report indicates that modest growth in retail spending can be expected over the next 5 years, with more growth in spending on non-food items than on food, and more growth in sales of specialist products than in generalist ones. The report forecasts a fall in the number of both retail firms and shops in the 1990s, with shops operated by small firms being most severely affected; an increase in the amount of part-time working; and a continuing increase in average shop size. The future overall pattern in the food retail sector in Scotland is that there could be a greater variety of formats with the market becoming more clearly segmented. The report indicates that the implications of these trends for planning are wide-ranging. Inter-urban competition to attract retailers and hence consumers is likely to become stronger as floorspace increases and there will be pressure on towns to respond to the needs and changes of demand if they are to retain their retail positions. Some of the intra-urban implications of the trends are that:

- town centres will retain their importance, but with smaller retail cores, an increased retail/leisure component; and the possibilty of commercial blight in secondary areas
- edge-of-town and out-of-centre developments will increase in importance
- individually sited stores will sustain their importance but some will be reused by other retailers and change function (often to discount formats)
- traditional suburban shopping centres will decline in importance, largely through loss of small shops and the effects of commercial blight.

The report considers that EC policies are likely to have an increasing influence on the pattern of retail provision. These include packaging and recycling requirements and initiatives concerned with environmental improvements. It admits, however, that there is a great deal of uncertainty about the relationship between retail planning policy and broader environmental policies.[32]

In an article from 1994 Walsh went so far as to say, "if statistics tell a story, then the retailing figures for the past ten years are a depressing tale of woe for British town centres. The rapid development of out-of-town retailing has had a major impact on town centres. In 1991 around 17% of all retail sales occurred out-of-town, compared with under 5% in 1980. There has meanwhile been a 12% fall in town centre shop numbers, coming in food specialists, hardware, furniture and electrical shops.

In 1994 three quarters of shopping floorspace was still found in town centres, but there were planning permissions outstanding or developments under construction for a further 59.5 mft^2. out of town, compared with 36.5 mft^2. on the high street. Add to such moves the growing popularity of convenience shops attached to petrol stations, the continuing development of retailing at airports and railway stations, along with the coming of the new American-style discount out-of-town warehouse and factory 'clubs', and you might begin to despair at the difficult task town centres face. While the latest government planning policy guidance and advice (PPGs 6 & 13) may be actively seeking to address the problem – by putting a strong emphasis on locating further development in town centres – evolving trends in retailing look set to make it increasingly difficult for many places, particularly smaller market towns, to retain their traditional shopping role."[33]

But, according to Walsh, traditional high streets are certainly not taking the challenge lying down. Many town centres are responding to the need to revive and survive. Indeed, whilst in the past one of the problems had been insufficient investment in town centres by hard-pressed local authorities, resulting in an image of decay and neglect, a large number of councils are now actively working at enhancing their high street shopping environments through major pedestrianisation and environmental improvement schemes, traffic calming measures, and the introduction of effective town centre management and promotion.

But the Environment Committee report has highlighted how the agenda prompted by PPGs 6 and 13 has left unanswered questions on the issue of accessibility. While out-of-town shopping centres lure shoppers with extensive (usually free) car parking, traffic pressures have been prompting clampdowns on car parking in many urban areas. Just how significant is the provision of parking to town centre success is still open to debate, however. Despite these fears, a study by Environ, the co-ordinators of Leicester's environmental city project, found no correlation between the amount and price of parking provision and shop vacancy rates. It concluded that the quality of the physical environment in a city centre had more influence on its success.

Along with the issue of accessibility, perhaps as crucial to the future of town centre retailing is the issue of role definition and market position. As Paul Joyce, director of store development for Boots the Chemist, stated at a conference on retail development in town centres, some town centres have a huge job to do to get themselves competitively advantaged and may have to settle for a lesser role than in the past. "They can still look to being the best in their redefined role. Other towns need to change less but must do so before the rot sets in," he warned. Boots, who have 80% of their stores in town centres, are leading the way in supporting a number of positive initiatives around the country aimed at town centre retail regeneration.

Professor David Locke, planning advisor to the Department of Environment, raised the issue of creating more specialist, locally distinctive shopping areas as a possible way forward for towns. Speaking at the Urban Design Group conference in September 1994, he said he was investigating ways of developing more variety and difference in town centres. "One of the factors limiting the process at present is the lack of variety in tenure and unit sizes," he commented. There were some lessons to be learnt from Europe, he believed, where town centres had encouraged more of a mixture of multiples and smaller shops in town centres. Given the importance of role definition and niche marketing, many local authorities are now actively researching in detail the health of their town centres and how best to develop their retailing futures.

For instance, Selby District Council appointed consultants Erdman Lewis to undertake a study on retailing in the area, focussing on the three main centres of Selby, Tadcaster and Sherburn-in-Elmet, which had all lost trade to nearby competitive centres York, Doncaster and Leeds. John Stockdale, director at Erdman Lewis, says the key aim of such studies is to assess the need for further retail provision and to inform future planning policy for the area using both quantitative and qualitative methods. Stockdale says small market towns have been hit particularly hard by out-of-town retailing in recent years. While in the 1980s nearly all foodstores over 20,000 sq. ft. were developed in towns with populations over 30,000, since 1990 a quarter of new stores have been developed in towns with smaller populations. Many local authorities were now recognising the need for specialist advice in order to draw up successful revival strategies. "Retailing is changing fast and local authorities need assistance in understanding its dynamic nature and how to keep competitive," he says.

The idea that the role of the town centre is changing and should now cater for a particular type of consumer is certainly reflected in Sainsbury's strategy. In 1994 Sainsbury's opened three pilot 'Central' stores. The first opened in Chelmsford, followed by Exeter and Epsom. Unlike the Tesco 'Metro' concept, which involves either developing new stores or taking space in existing or proposed shopping centres, the 'Central' stores all involve the total refurbishment and remerchandising of an existing Sainsbury's store. The aim is to tailor the stores more to the particular types of customers who regularly shop in town centres for food and who normally represent small households.

As well as the efforts of local authorities and individual retailers, there is some other support in the battle to maintain traditional town centres. The Civic Trust Regeneration Unit's (CTRU) Centre Vision programme, supported by Boots the Chemist and the Department of Environment, has tried to forge new roles for town centres hit by the recession and the effects of out-of-town retailing. When Walsh was writing the programme had only been in operation for a year but had already completed reports for Falmouth in Cornwall and Eccles in Lancashire, along with other towns such as Blackburn, Huddersfield, Dudley and Doncaster. Marketing manager for CTRU, Sarah Peasley, said the studies completed so far highlighted the growing importance of introducing town centre management and co-ordinated marketing and promotion of town centres. Many towns, she feels, have neglected attractive historic buildings in their town centres. "Restoring these can be an important part of the regeneration process." Developing local distinctiveness, through such initiatives as the development and promotion of specialist markets, is also vital in the battle to remain competitive, maintains Peasley. Enhancement of the town centre environment as a safe and attractive place to shop is seen as an important first step towards building new retailing roles. Pedestrianisation is an increasingly popular tool in the process. Following the pedestrianisation of Reading town centre the manager, Peter Fieldhouse, commented: "it is clear that town centres are at a turning point. The government is attempting to exercise some degree of balance, but, at the end of the day, the responsibility for the town centres' fight for survival rests with themselves."

Loxton has considered ways in which town planners can best improve upon the retail landscape.[34] He does this by reviewing various success stories, including classic examples of pedestrianisation seen in places such as Norwich city centre. He offers advice on how town centres can offset the negative impact of out-of-town developments. He also looks at the positive aspects of the trend towards out-of-town retailing, considered through the eyes of the landscape planner. As he says, new out-of-town shopping centres are characterised by large car parks and tree-lined avenues, with vast external and internal spaces offering a range of goods and products. These centres often have a high standard of external design which perhaps lacks some of the intimacy and variety so often found in the old town centres but does offer the opportunity for the designer to provide bold statements.

The Metro Centre in Newcastle is cited as the best known example of a major out-of-town shopping centre which, quite rightly, has forged a character of its own with no reference to any historical or contextual constraints. The landscaped design complements the more functional requirements of the scheme in a bold and uncompromising manner.

Loxton feels the pedestrianized schemes associated with the late 1970s and early 1980s have often resulted in over-design, a great clutter and profusion of street furniture, signs and other artefacts. He sees the revitalization of town centres and shopping centres and shopping streets as an increasing challenge. The out-of-town shopping centre, although often dramatic in concept, requires the same care and attention to detail if success is to be realized. The use of more natural materials in combination with the many excellent concrete products now available provides designs which will be durable and meet the changing fashions and expectations of a more demanding public. The overall lesson from the schemes reviewed by Loxton is that quality rather quantity leads to the ultimate success over time.

Gregory has attempted to show how a particular retailer, WH Smith, has decided to become more involved in local planning in order to preserve the character of the high street whilst at the same time improving its' image in the community.[35] The town in question is Eastleigh in Hampshire where a member of staff at WH Smith has been seconded to become town centre manager. The newly created post is the focal point of a partnership project aimed at enhancing Eastleigh's role as a retail and commercial centre. A consultation document, *Eastleigh Town Centre into the 1990s*, was produced with areas for discussion such as layout, appearance, development, access, parking and management.

WH Smith's interest in the project was summed up in a message from Lawrence James, retail sales director, in the publication *Commitment to the Community* "the traditional High Street has character, and there is no surer way to find out what is distinctive about a particular town than to head for its centre – where the shops are. High streets and town centres are particularly important to WH Smith, because that is where you find most of our shops." He added, "however, we cannot take town centres for granted. They have competition from other kinds of retail environments, such as hypermarkets and increasingly mail order shopping. It's in our interests to make town centres thrive, and we can help do that."

WH Smith identified the benefits of being involved in the local partnership as follows:

- increasing WH Smith's influence on the decisions and policy-making which affect trade in town centres
- developing a positive reputation and high street profile for WH Smith
- increasing sales by making the town centre a better place to shop
- preventing a decline in town-centre shopping
- encouraging local branch initiative
- providing opportunities to develop branch managers
- helping to remove obstacles to trade.

The important role of town centre management was emphasised with the publication of the Government's policy planning guidance notes, by ministerial statements and by the House of Commons environment committee report on shopping centres. A great deal has also been written on how schemes should be progressed. It is clear, however, that no two towns are alike and that whilst guidelines and best practice can be demonstrated, each town needs to develop its own approach to meet its particular situation. This is where WH Smith feels it can make an important contribution to the development of the local community.

The 1997 *Retail Marketing Yearbook*, produced by Verdict, raises a number of issues currently facing the retail trade.[36] Of particular interest is the contribution by Sue Wheldon, Retail Design Director of BDG McColl, entitled '*Regenerating the Retail Environment*'. Wheldon considers how retailers should deal with their current property portfolios in the light of changing retail distribution channels and shopping locations. Should they relocate to newer locations, recycle tired or redundant sites with new concept stores or offload them on to newcomers to the retail sector, such as the major brand product manufacturers? To date, the majority of retailers have operated out of shops and market places. Until the latter part of this century these shops were located in the high streets of towns and villages – generally where people live and work. More recently out-of-town shopping malls, retail parks, factory outlets and transport hubs have seen the main thrust of retail development in the Western world. Now, in the late 1990s, shoppers do not even need to leave their homes:

- television channels dedicated to home shopping exist across Europe
- retail websites on the Internet offer online shopping
- catalogue shopping and home delivery services are available for most durable and non-durable products.

These choices are both exciting and daunting for the customer, but for the retailer they create dilemmas – should they expand their offer to include some or all of these new retailing formats? If so, how? What impact will they have on the traditional retail property portfolio? Wheldon highlights other considerations:

- the growth of transport hub retailing at bus and railway stations, airports, petrol stations, ports and other transit areas requires new site acquisitions or modular concession units capable of being implanted into these host environments
- Internet and catalogue shopping requires Call Centres and warehouse storage space, which can often be created by internally reconfiguring and reducing the retail trading areas in existing sites. It is also possible to incorporate the now redundant in-store warehouse areas, which have been vacated in favour of retailers' new central distribution outlets
- however, stores in shopping centres, retail parks and high streets form the core of a retailer's current property portfolio. It is in these locations that they have the potential to regenerate sites with tired trading formats in order to keep ahead of the competition.

According to Verdict, the greatest impact on UK retailers' property portfolios in the past 16 years has been caused by the move out-of-town, where sales today account for 32% of all UK retail sales – up from 4.6% in 1980. Verdict also estimates that high streets currently account for 50% of all sales, down from 56% in 1980.

Some retailers have expanded their property estates by opening in the newer out-of-town locations in the 1980s and early 1990s, whilst still retaining stores in the high street. Customers have been drawn to out-of-town and mall shopping locations because of easy access by car, free parking, comfortable environments protected from the elements and, increasingly, by the opportunity of enjoying a leisure experience. However, in the late 1990s several factors have started to reverse this trend. As we have seen, government planning laws have restricted further out-of-town retail development both to encourage the revival of the high street and to discourage travel by car. In the eyes of Verdict, "time famine has become the modern day scourge, and customers are once more using the quick and easy shopping option – their local high street."[37]

Retailers again face the need to invest in their increasingly more varied and complex portfolios in order to keep up with these latest trends. A Healey & Baker survey of shopping habits concludes that the customer of the late 1990s considers convenience to be the most important factor when choosing where to shop. The survey found that 50% of shoppers chose their local neighbourhood stores as the most popular shopping locations, both because of convenience and because of friendly service. Retailers can take heart from these messages. Customers will still travel out-of-town for ease of parking and the leisure shopping experience, but they will continue to use their local neighbourhood stores for convenience.

Wheldon sees the challenge for retailers to tailor their property portfolio into a series of different store formats, each of which can comfortably co-exist under one retailing umbrella. Tesco is held-up as a good example of a retailer which has successfully added to and recycled its property in order to cater for customers in all of the latest retailing locations, using a series of different store formats:

- hypermarkets
- out-of-town superstores
- supermarkets in town and on the edge of town
- express stores in transport hubs
- metro stores in convenience and high density locations.

Once other retailers have followed the Tesco example and successfully catered for customers in all key locations, Wheldon believes the next major challenge will be to cater for the social needs of the growing number of people who work alone at home, plus those who travel extensively for business. These people are likely to shop for basic goods on the Internet. When they do go out to shop, it will be as much for social interaction as for their purchases.

Wheldon believes "the shopping centre of the future will satisfy a real social need, giving customers an opportunity for human interaction in their leisure time. It is likely that groceries and basic household items will have been delivered to their homes. When they go out to shop, it will be for higher value household goods, to try on the latest clothing fashions and to test the latest electrical and electronic goods. As these outings will be less frequent than today, the retailer and leisure operator will need to make the experience memorable and exciting. Retailers will need to consider operating partnerships from within the leisure sector to ensure delivery of this exciting and stimulating experience."[38]

In the UK, it is unlikely that planning restrictions on out-of-town retail development will be lifted in the near future. It will therefore be necessary for retailers and developers to recycle and reconfigure existing developments to cater for the newly merged retail and leisure sectors. Surrounding external spaces which include car parks may be used more creatively than now, either as drive-in cinemas and theatres or for seasonal barbecues, concerts and other events. The American food retailer, Stu Lennard, has successfully introduced evening events in his Connecticut store car parks, erecting marquees for Halloween cook-outs and for mass-selling of seasonal products such as Christmas trees. The challenge to architects and retail developers in the future will be to create shopping centres and retail parks which are flexible enough within their internal layouts to cater for retailers' changing spatial needs.

The high street of the future presents different opportunities for retailers and the greatest potential for regenerating redundant property. The smaller human scale of the high street environment will have its own appeal as it will still be close to where people live and work. The convenience and ease of shopping in this local environment will be a major bonus to the customer of the future. Local shops are like local pubs: they feel secure in an ever-changing world. The sense of belonging to a community will be very important to the home worker of the future. The retail and leisure mix of the future high street will undoubtedly change. The overall emphasis of the high street will become that of "making life easy", that is, offering goods and services for everybody's day-to-day needs. It will also be a place for providing advance information about entertainment, fashion and other more expensive products available in the nearby retail and leisure centres.

Wheldon imagines the customer on the future 'Easy High Street' will find most of the following:

- fresh produce and foodstuffs retailers, trading or vending 24 hours a day and offering home delivery

- catalogue shops, advertising products available in the larger out-of-town stores
- healthcare outlets, selling curative and preventative health products, as well as giving advice and holding fitness classes and consultations
- money shops and financial advice centres tailored to different age groups
- commercial crèches and childcare outlets with cafés
- business centres/self-service hotels for the visitor and home worker, a place to hold meetings, attend global video conferences and use specialist equipment
- Internet cafés with personal computer banking, on-line shopping and electronic games, all in a social environment
- branded entertainment retailers offering music, books and other hobby products
- service retailers including hairdressers, dry cleaners, laundries, newsagents and travel shops
- pubs, wine bars, sports cafés and restaurants.

This may not sound like your average high street today but Wheldon feels optimistic that this can become a reality in the not too distant future. Supermarkets in the high street will have the opportunity of offering added value to customers through promoting leisure events in-store, focusing for example on music nights and singles evenings for the local young and old. As the population ages, retailers will have to become more sensitive to their needs, perhaps by providing vehicle collection and delivery back home to the customers who lack mobility but still enjoy the shopping experience in the familiar high street.

Wheldon feels that retail designers such as BDG McColl have a responsibility to their clients and must be sensitive both to their needs today and their vision for the future. She concludes that whilst the choices and challenges facing retailers in the millenium may be enormous, the potential for regeneration is equally great. The regeneration of out-of-date or redundant retail property in existing shopping centres and the high street has already begun. This, together with the merging of the retail and leisure sectors, is seen as the most exciting opportunity facing retailers today.

Wheldon's is one of a number of commentaries that have seen the traditional high street fighting back against out-of-town developments. In reality, the high street trader and the consumer have yet to be convinced. For example, a recent report which branded Leighton Buzzard one of the most successful high streets because of its high rents was slammed by the town's traders. According to research by property consultants Colliers Erdman Lewis, the centre has not been affected by out-of-town retail parks with rents rising 100% in the past decade. They claim this is a measure of the town centre's success. Traders say this is ridiculous. In the past few years dozens of shops have closed, many of them well established family firms such as George Ort's the bakers and S G Willis and Sons greengrocers. But despite the closures, the town is in the top 10 of the best rental rankings in the region. The research, which concentrates on non-food shopping, reveals the best performing high streets in the South East are those with relatively more out-of-town shopping nearby.

Topping the list of best performing high streets was Milton Keynes which trebled its rents for tenants. In Leighton Buzzard's Bossard Centre many shops have closed down – reeling at the presence of edge-of-town superstores Tesco and Safeway. The Town and District Councils are so concerned about the lack of shops they have asked town centre manager Georgina Whyatt to compile a promotion package urging retailers to open shops in the town. Chamber of Trade chairman Diane Bradfield was shocked to hear the survey results. She said: "This is ridiculous. I think it is affecting the town and continuing to do so. You only have to look around at the number of empty shops. Rising overheads and loss of business to out-of-town supermarkets are the prime reasons." Town Centre manager Whyatt confirmed the generally held view that the survey by Colliers Erdman Lewis "seemed an illogical way to measure the town's success."

Mintel, the consumer market research publisher, has produced a number of reports on the future of retailing. As well as regular updates in the Mintel series *Retail Intelligence*, these will often appear as separate 'Special Reports'. In 1995 Mintel published the *Survival of the High Street*, which charts the development of retail selling space by looking at the backgound issues involved in changing the face of town and city centres.[39] The report looks in detail at the retail attraction for the various types of shopper and at the attraction of shopping locally. Finally, the outlook for the future is discussed. This report was followed in 1997 by *Shopping Centres*, in which Mintel provide a detailed analysis of the development of shopping centres in the UK.[40] There is an outline of the factors influencing shopping centre development, a look at out-of-town regional shopping centres and the role and impact of shopping centres on other shopping locations. The report offers advice on improving the attractiveness of large shopping centres and comments on important issues such as occupancy and marketing and operations management. Finally, Mintel ponder the future for shopping centres.

Figures from the international shop agents Hillier Parker show official restrictions on out-of-town shopping developments beginning to take effect; new-scheme-proposals for retail parks are down by 20% on 1996, although space under construction is sharply up as projects in a more liberal era come to fruition. Planning restraints are being applied more vigorously in the south, Hillier Parker finds, leaving retail park development heavily biased towards northern parts. Mr Nick Raynsford, Minister for London and Construction, has rejected yet more press rumours that the Government was a closet liberal on this topic; the categorical message, delivered at a British Council of Shopping Centres Conference, was that there would be no lifting of the brakes on either new out-of-town developments or extensions to existing centres. This last piece of intelligence comes as particularly bad news to the developers of Gateshead Metro Centre who have advanced the argument that the latest generation of out-of-town regional centres were now so much part of the social fabric that they should be treated for planning purposes in the same way as traditional centres.

Multiples need less than half the stores to reach the same number of non-food shoppers than they did 25 years ago, according to a survey of consumer habits in the UK. The *National Survey of Local Shopping Patterns*, commissioned by Hillier Parker, reveals that retailers can reach half the UK's population with stores in 73 key locations out of the country's 3,000-plus trading areas. This compares to the early 1970s when it took more than 200 trading locations nationally to attract similar numbers.

The survey, which concentrated on comparison goods shoppers in the non-food sector, also confirmed the growing trend towards retailers looking for larger sites in fewer locations. Hillier Parker's head of retail research, Mark Teale, said both independents and smaller high streets were losing out to the retail trend for critical mass. However, he added, the change is gradual because the number of larger sites in the key trading locations is limited, and retailers often have long lease commitments to prevent them from off-loading older, smaller units. Non-food shopping remains firmly rooted in town and city-centre locations, rather than out-of-town, according to the report. The top ten shopping destinations are London's West End, Glasgow, Leeds, Manchester, Birmingham, Newcastle, Edinburgh, Liverpool, Nottingham and Cardiff. The report pinpointed Sheffield's Meadowhall as the most popular out-of-town centre, 18th in the rankings, Lakeside is 19th, followed by the Metro Centre (24th) and Merry Hill, Dudley (27th).

The government produced Planning Policy Guidance notes have put great emphasis on town centre management. One of the most popular methods of improvement to existing town centres has been pedestrianisation. As part of a series of policy reviews, Lincolnshire County Council commissioned research to establish whether money spent on pedestrianisation and other town centre improvements was money well spent. The results of a survey of 180 businesses trading there before their street was pedestrianised indicated that 44% of all traders believed that pedestrianisation had increased their trade. Only 14% identified a decrease following pedestrianisation with the remainder reporting no effect or did not know.[41] Town centre management and promotion is rising on the local agenda in Lincolnshire, as elsewhere, perhaps given new impetus by PPG13 and by other developments such as the DoT bypass demonstration projects and the more proactive attitude of some of the large multiples. Comprehensive studies of local opinion in Louth and Sleaford have helped shape local shopping centre developments. For example, in Louth a survey of 375 shoppers showed that traffic and parking figured low in the minds of shoppers, who were more concerned with the whole shopping experience than merely the mechanics of getting to the shops, and indicated local preference for a more pedestrian-friendly town centre without full pedestrianisation.

Those who try to alter town centres often find they have embarked on a long and controversial path. Practitioners are often encouraged to listen to public opinion but not always can a true cross-section of opinion be heard. It was found that actively seeking out public views provided valuable insight and also helped build consensus –perhaps leading to better decisions!

Most shopping centres and pedestrianised areas are designed with access in mind. A report by Armitage looks at how many town centre managers are taking advantage of this and providing wheelchairs for disabled shoppers.[42] 'Shopmobility' is a straightforward concept. It improves the ability of disabled people to use facilities at shopping malls and pedestrianised areas in town centres through the provision of wheelchairs and pavement vehicles. The service is generally free or at very low cost to users, and there are now about 130 schemes in the UK.

Prompted by the growth in large shopping complexes and town centre pedestrianisation, shopmobility has begun to address the problems these developments create for disabled people. The National Federation of Shopmobility describes it as 'providing equal opportunity and participation in the shopping experience.' Shopmobility is becoming accepted as part of sound practice in town centre management. So much so that it is spreading to other places where significant numbers of people need to get around a car-free area.

Freeborn has profiled the company Capital Shopping Centres (CSC), responsible for Lakeside, Thurrock, Harlequin Centre, Watford and the Metro Centre in Gateshead.[43] He says, "the government can wring its hands about Britain's starving high streets. CSC has already changed the geography of South East England." The distinctive feature of CSC's management approach is its appetite for turnover-related rents. CSC are on the look-out for additions to their portfolio – the key criteria is dominance in a large catchment area. Their main hopes for the future lie in the continued growth of the Lakeside and Metro Centre developments.

Brignull has argued that "on the face of it, the high street is our most democratic institution. We vote there at least once a week and not just with our feet but with our purses. Those shops which supply our needs thrive, those that don't get boarded over. Cruel but fair." He believes, however, that the average traditional high street has become too predictable, too mundane. Visit any town in the country, he argues, and you will be confronted with the same combination of stores, building societies and fast food chains. "The high street", says Brignull, "is among our biggest cultural influences, far more influential than the theatre or literature. But it has changed – and without a referendum. It is time for councils and planning officers to positively discriminate in favour of the high street, to give rate holidays to shops we need and to load those we don't."[44] Whilst the high street has begun the major task of regaining custom lost during the out-of-town retailing explosion, it clearly has a long way to go if it is to win the battle.

References

1   Harris R, *Whither the high street?*, London, Gerald Eve Research, 1995.

2   Couch H, Are Town Centres Really Declining?, *Estates Gazette*, Issue 9602, 1996 p101-103.

3   Wrigley N, 1998, "Understanding store development programmes in post-property-crisis UK food retailing", *Environment and Planning* A, 30, 15-35.

4   Jenkins S, 1997, *The Times*, 19 April, 20.

5   Guy C M, 1998, "Alternative-use valuation, open A1 planning consent, and the development of retail parks", *Environment and Planning* A, 30, 37-47.

6   Guy C M, 1998, "'High street' retailing in off-centre retail parks: a review of the effectiveness of land use planning policies", *Town Planning Review*, 69 (3), 291-313.

7   ibid.

8   Langston P, Clarke G P, Clarke D B, 1998, "Retail saturation: the debate in the mid-1990s", *Environment and Planning A*, 30, 49-66.

9   Langston P, Clarke G P, Clarke D B, 1997, "Retail saturation, retail location and retail competition: and analysis of British food retailing", *Environment and Planning* A, 29, 77-104.

10 UK has room for more big stores, *The Times*, 16/6/97

11 URBED (Urban and Economic Development Group) *Town Centre Partnerships: a survey of good practice and report of an action research project*: a report for the Association of Town Centre Management – London: Department of the Environment, 1997.

12 Raven, H. and Lang, T. *Off our Trolleys?: food retailing and the hypermarket economy*, – London: Institute for Public Policy Research, 1995.

13 ibid.

14 ibid.

15 ibid.

16 Guy, C.M. Official Publications on Retail Development: a Review Article, *Planning Practice and Research*, Vol.11, No.2, 227-234, 1996.

17 ibid.

18 ibid.

19 Burke, T. Competition Issues 1995/96: Open When You Like, but not Where You Like, *Retail World*, Autumn 1996, p.3-4.

20 ibid.

21 Department of the Environment. *Environment Select Committee Inquiry: Shopping Centres and their Future* – London: Department of the Environment, 1994.

22 Department of the Environment. *The Government's Response to the Fourth Report from the House of Commons Select Committee on the Environment: Shopping Centres and their Future* – London: HMSO, 1995.

23 Urban and Economic Development Group (URBED). *Vital and Viable Town Centres: Meeting the Challenge* – London: HMSO, 1994.

24 BDP Planning and Oxford Institute of Retail Management. *The Effects of Major Out of Town Retail Development* – London: HMSO, 1992.

25 Department of the Environment. *Consultation Draft: Planning Policy Guidance 6: Town Centres and Retail Developments* – London: Department of the Environment, 1995.

26 Department of the Environment and Department of Transport. *Planning Policy Guidance 13: Transport* – London: HMSO, 1994.

27 Department of the Environment and Welsh Office. *Planning Policy Guidance 6: Major Retail Development* – London: HMSO, 1988.

28 Department of the Environment and Welsh Office. *Planning Policy Guidance 6: Town Centres and Retail Developments* – London: HMSO, 1993.

29 Guy, C.M. *The Retail Development Process* – London: Routledge, 1994.

30. House of Commons Environment Committee. *Fourth Report: Shopping Centres and Their Futures* – London: HMSO, 1994.

31 Development Department, Scottish Office. *National Planning Policy Guidance NPPG 8: Retailing* – Edinburgh: 1996.

32 Dawson J, *Review of Retailing Trends* – Edinburgh: Scottish Office, 1994.

33 Walsh, B., 'Do Town Centres Need a New Retail Role?' *Urban Street Environment*, Oct/Nov 1994, p10-15.

34 Loxton, M. 'The Landscape of Retail', *Built Environment* V.21, no.1, p45-53.

35 Gregory, J. 'The Retail Perspective', *Municipal Journal*, No.28, 1995, p24-25.

36 *Retail Marketing Yearbook* – London: Verdict, 1997.

37 ibid.

38 ibid.

39 Mintel, *Survival of the High Street*, Special Report – London, 1995.

40 Mintel, *Shopping Centres*, Special Report – London, 1997.

41 Watson J. 'Trading spaces', *Surveyor*, 23 November 1995, p26-29.

42 Armitage, R. 'Access to the consumer world', *Surveyor*, 4 April 1996, p20-22,

43 Freeborn T. 'CSC – shopping for success' *Estates Gazette*, 20 January 1996, p58-61.

44 Brignull T, 'High streets from hell', *Guardian*, 5/11/97.

2. Moving Out-of-Town – Driving the Shopper

Richard Hayward and Sue McGlynn of the Joint Centre for Urban Design, Oxford Brookes University, have described out-of-town shopping as "lakeside and bucolic in its built form, serving the tile, thatch and dovecots of new urban cottagery."[1] In considering if we get the town centres we deserve, they state "great and reasonable play is made for the town centre over the out-of-town centre, in that the former is essentially more sustainable and more democratic in terms of access and synergetic support for complementary cultural and other infrastructure: public offices, healthcare and so on. Yet the current problem shared by out-of-town and downtown centres is the mutual quest for control and maximisation of market opportunities." Hayward and McGlynn contribute some interesting thoughts on the urban dimension involved in the town centre/edge-of-town/out-of-town shopping debate.

They review much of the key report literature that has appeared in recent years. The report of the House of Commons Environment Committee on *Shopping Centres and Their Future* provides an excellent summary of the views of all the major stakeholders in retail planning and development. At the same time it is an excellent source for those who want to find out easily and reliably what has been happening in the UK retail sector over the last 20 years, bringing together as it does an enormous amount of material from widely disparate expert sources. The Committee make detailed recommendations, including a review of planning gain guidance; a review of PPGs 6 and 13 to reconcile the conflict over car parking in town centres; and a handbook for planning inspectors to ensure consistency of decision making. The report states that existing town and district centres need to be promoted as attractive and viable places in which to shop, and at the same time planning controls must restrict out-of-town developments, particularly retail parks and the new retail concepts such as factory outlets and warehouse clubs. Hayward and McGlynn regard the subsequent study, *Vital and Viable Town Centres*, as a landmark publication. It "should be praised for not purporting to have 'the answers', but the consistent pattern of inconclusively reviewing the balance of different approaches is enervating, particularly for those who must act and cannot afford the luxury simply of philosophical reflection." In conclusion, they believe the potential weaknesses of town centre management "are that they acknowledge little life beyond retailing and seldom aspire higher than the housekeeping role that may exceed the janitorial, but is essentially domestic and introverted."[2]

The Royal Institution of Chartered Surveyors (RICS) has said that any debate on out-of-town shopping must start from an understanding of the factors that gave rise to it.[3] These include the difficulties of access to and within town centres, changes in lifestyle, the growth of DIY, increasing demand for bulky consumer goods and increased personal mobility. According to the RICS, these factors will continue to create a demand for out-of-town shopping facilities. The RICS is also critical of the notion implicit in PPG 6 that stopping developments from happening out-of-town will necessarily stimulate developments in town centres. The belief is that "if the right conditions do not exist in town centres then development will simply not happen." An additional view is that an out-of-town location may sometimes be the best choice on environmental and other grounds and there is a real concern that PPG 6 could create insurmountable obstacles to out-of-town development.

The proceedings of the 1995 Vision for London Symposium has an interesting synopsis of responses from, amongst others, 'the retailer' Martin Wright of Marks & Spencer and 'the property owner' William McKee of the British Property Federation.

Wright believes "retailers operate a 'We'll give it to you where you want it policy' – if customers want it out-of-town then we will be forced to give it to them out-of-town." McKee adds that "shopping by computer will take 20% of trade from high streets over the next 20 years." The Government perspective is represented by the Rt Hon John Gummer. In his speech he touches upon planning permission for out-of-town shopping centres, stating that "it is probably easy if you have got a small town and somebody wants to build outside on the green belt. You know which is an out-of-town shopping centre and which is an in-centre shopping centre. But it is very much harder when you are talking about whether you should build on the old gas works which is 200 yards from the end of a very tatty shopping centre. That is the kind of thing we (i.e. local government and retailers) need to work through together."[4]

A new and interesting dimension to the battle between town and country is looming. John Bryson, general manager of the Metro Centre, is trying to convince the Government that the project he has nurtured for 11 years on the edge of Gateshead has evolved into something much bigger than just an out-of-town shopping centre. "We have now become a town in our own right," he says. "In terms of economic generation (an estimated annual total 'spend' of £800 million) we are equal to a city the size of Oxford. We might have no museums or libraries, but we have reached a critical point where people are now saying 'you now meet all our needs'."

It is, say critics, a clever ploy to pressure the Government into re-designating the UK's big four shopping centres – Gateshead, Sheffield, Dudley and Thurrock – by dropping the unhelpful out-of-town tag, with all its implications of raping the countryside and destroying traditional shopping areas, so that expansion plans can be pushed through. Four other shopping complexes – near Glasgow, Bristol, Manchester and Dartford – are being built at a combined cost of almost £2 billion, while more are in the pipeline. The plans will challenge the fragile policy, agreed by the last Government, to curb out-of-town growth. The re-designation plans have alarmed the Council for the Protection of Rural England. "It's hard to believe they're serious," says Tony Burton, the organisation's assistant director. "They're not real town centres. They don't provide a full range of services. They've no culture, no history and they're hugely reliant on the motor car."

But serious they are – although Gateshead's planning committee only approved the Metro Centre's £50 million expansion by one vote. Now the plan has been passed for a final decision to the Deputy Prime Minister, John Prescott, who heads the Department of the Environment, Transport and the Regions. Few doubt his determination to curb car use, but developers, who became exasperated with John Gummer sense a softening attitude in Downing Street and are now coming forward with bigger expansion plans. The Lakeside complex, in Thurrock, Essex, wants to grow to compete with a second wave of centres – in its case, an even bigger centre, the Bluewater development, two miles away beside the A2 in Kent. It promises to be the largest in Britain when completed in 1999, with over 300 shops and 13,000 parking spaces. Peter Walicknowski, European chief executive of Bluewater's developers, Australian company Land Lease, says: "It looks like out-of-town now but in 10 years time it will be something quite different." Over 5,000 houses are planned a few hundred metres away, and 20,000 more are likely in the surrounding area – creating what Kent county council calls a "new town in all but name."

At 1.5km across, 50m in depth and with a surface area of 100 hectares, cement manufacturer Blue Circle's old West Quarry, near Dartford, was one of the country's larger empty holes in the ground. But the company had the luck to win planning permission to turn this hole into a giant retail centre, just before planning policy moved decisively against out-of-town shopping. The result is one of the largest construction projects in the UK, combined with a complex reconstruction and realignment of surrounding roads. Bluewater was one of the last out-of-town retail developments to gain planning permission before the change in planning policy. Mark Smulian has considered the likely effects on existing centres. As he says, "the Thurrock Lakeside shopping complex is close enough to be visible from Bluewater across the Thames. While Bluewater may well kill off custom that Lakeside now attracts from Kent, it is unlikely to do fundamental damage to its heavily-used northern neighbour, which can draw on a catchment area in Essex and east London. Land Lease [the property developer] sees its main competitors as the large stores of central London, Bromley and Croydon, rather than the local centres in Dartford and Gravesend. It argues that there is no major shopping centre in the county."[5]

In 1998 the Merry Hill shopping centre, in Dudley, the West Midlands, tried – and failed – to become, in effect, the new town centre for the area. It wanted a near 50% expansion, but a planning inspector ruled it did not constitute a town centre "at least yet." But Nigel Hugill, managing director of the centre's developers, Chelsfield, says: "I am quite sure we will succeed. It's just a question of time." Table 2.1 indicates the development plans in the pipeline for the UK's major shopping centres.

The real 'store wars' are taking place in country towns across the country. In historic Ludlow, for example, many of the locals are aghast at the thought of a new Tesco store nestling amongst the listed buildings. Here it took John Prescott, Secretary of State for Environment, Transport and the Regions, just 14 days to do what the Tory's Environment Secretary, John Gummer, declined to do in four years: to lift the restriction on Tesco building a 23,200 sq-ft "neighbourhood food store" on the site where pale-faced Herefords once changed hands. Ludlow now has an out-of-town cattle market. It will have a large supermarket "in town", according to Nicole Lander, Tesco's corporate affairs manager, or "on the edge of town", according to local resident Sir Julian Critchley and his fellow members of the Civic Society. Thanks to planning guidelines on superstores bequeathed by John Gummer, there are likely to be more of these 'neighbourhood stores' built during the next few years. "Because shopping patterns have changed, we're looking for sites in smaller places than we would have done five years ago," says Lander. "That's true of Sainsbury's and our other rivals as well. Ludlow is very important to us." The general belief is that if they can get it right in Ludlow, they can get it right anywhere.[6]

Table 2.1 Major UK Shopping Centres – Development Plans

Shopping Centre	Size	Future Development
Lakeside (Thurrock)	350 shops; 1.3 million sq. ft.	Wants 20% expansion. Prescott to decide.
Metro Centre (Gateshead)	320 shops; 1.5 million sq. ft	Applied for 10% expansion. Plans with Prescott.
Meadowhall (Sheffield)	270 shops; 1.2 million sq. ft.	Preparing to expand.
Merry Hill (Dudley)	225 shops; 1.8 million sq. ft.	Expanded 1996. Plans to add another 50% rejected.
Bluewater (Dartford)	300+ shops; 1.6 million sq. ft.	Opening mid-1999.
Trafford Centre (Manchester)	300+ shops; 1.3 million sq. ft.	Opened 1998.
Cribbs Causeway (Bristol)	140 shops; 725,000 sq. ft.	Opened 1998.
Braehead (Glasgow)	100 shops; 600,000 sq. ft.	Opening mid-1999. Scotland's first big out-of-town centre.

(Source: *Guardian* 5/11/97)

In 1997 the much-maligned Milton Keynes was named as the best shopping centre in Britain. The 1.2 million square feet shopping mall under glass and concrete between the exotically named Midsummer and Silbury boulevards was judged to include the best shops, the best environment and the best facilities of the country's 900 shopping centres. Conrad Rowland, managing director of the consultancy Retail Directions, who produced the rankings, said: "From the consumer perspective, Milton Keynes is the best shopping centre in terms of quality of retailer." With its new status, the aisles will be buzzing even more in the future, although Retail Directions warns that there is plenty of new competition. Huge malls such as Bluewater at Dartford and Bristol's Cribbs Causeway, are adding 7 million square feet to Britain's shopping halls over the next couple of years.

The failure rate of retailers' appeals against planning refusals has reached 67% since Policy Planning Guidance 6 first underwent restrictive draft revision in July 1995, according to research by DTZ Debenham Thorpe. The Labour Government's stance has been even tougher, if anything, with an emphatic preference for edge-of-town and brown field sites. It has been suggested that the Government is contemplating the use of parking-slot-taxes to discourage car use in crowded city centres, and that its thinking could also extend to out-of-town centres to ensure an even playing field.

The latest Grimley/CBI survey of property trends finds retailers looking increasingly to suburban and/or freestanding locations for their expansion, at the expense of both out-of-town and town centre locations.[7] Whilst construction of new out-of-town shopping centre space has been at an all-time high during 1996 and 1997, no major shopping centres have been proposed this decade (all the current schemes working their way through the pipeline were originally proposed during the 1980s). With little in the way of new out-of-town scheme proposals, apart from factory outlet centres and small food anchored schemes, mainstream shopping centre development activity in out-of-town markets currently looks set to all but cease in 2001/2002, hence the scramble by retailers for representation in the handful of major out-of-town schemes due to be completed over the next 3-4 years.

There was a small increase in town centre located shopping scheme proposals during the first two quarters of 1997. Despite this increase there is, as yet, little evidence that the Government's PPG6 is boosting town centre development activity. At the end of June 1996 – for the first time on record – the amount of shopping centre space under construction in out-of-town markets actually exceeded that in town centres. The amount of shopping centre floorspace under construction in out-of-town markets is now nearly three times town centre levels. The premium placed on out-of-town space by retailers clearly remains very substantial.

Developers have sought to reduce risk by concentrating on schemes that are sufficiently large, in critical mass terms, to dominate local retail markets. Almost 40% of the shopping centre floorspace currently in the development pipeline, and over

80% of the space actually under construction, is accounted for by schemes of more than 40,000 sq.m. Only about 20% of existing shopping centre space nationally is located in schemes of more than 40,000 sq.m., so the current development bias towards larger scheme sizes is very marked. The trend is likely to continue in the medium term. The big out-of-town regional centres – Meadowhall, Lakeside, Metro Centre and Merry Hill having proved startlingly successful.

Hillier Parker report that scheduled completion totals need to be treated with extreme caution. A high proportion of projects, particularly town centre located schemes, fail to meet initially scheduled completion dates. Completion levels in 1997 were expected to total about 250,000 sq.m. Completions in 1998/1999 are expected to be well below 400,000 sq.m. in each year. Hillier Parker predict the year 2000 will mark the effective end of out-of-town regional shopping centre development in Britain.

Throughout the 1980s and the early 1990s the debate surrounding the comparative costs and benefits of town centre and out-of-town retail developments for consumers and to the environment has been a heated one. Informed by a largely puritanical view of consumerism, current Government policy tends towards the preservation of the traditional town centre. However, the actual evidence is far from conclusive and there is limited consumer research supporting this stance. Based on an interviewer-administered survey conducted during 1994 and 1995 to assess shoppers' opinions in both types of location in Preston, Alzubaidi et al have presented an examination of consumer perspectives and behaviour patterns among town centre and out-of-town shoppers.[8]

While in 1980 only 5% of sales took place through out-of-town retailing, by 1991 this had grown to 17% and the trend is towards further increases. MacDonald (1987) identified sustained population dispersal, accelerating technological change and the continuing evolution of retail forms as key driving factors in the continued growth of out-of-town retailing.[9] Despite the many positive arguments in favour of out-of-town retailing, most proposals for out-of-town centres are rejected. The early 1990s saw a further tightening of government policy in this area. In *Planning Policy Guidance Note 6, Town Centres and Retail Developments*, a shift in government policy becomes apparent towards the protection of town centres and the discouragement of out-of-town developments. The background to this official perspective is shown by the Department of the Environment (1994, pp.37-8) findings: "...our survey of local authority planning officers established that 155 of market and 285 of suburban town centres also feel they are declining... Overall, 36% of respondents said that competition from an out-of-town or edge-of-town development was a major problem for their centre and 49% that it was a minor problem."

Thomas and Bromley (1993) point to an emergent polarization of shopping behaviour, with shopping centres meeting the needs of the affluent car-owning part of the population and town centres being used by the less mobile and for top-up shopping.[10] The principle of top-up shopping seems a way to satisfy both areas of demand, and retailers like Tesco are considering the principle as a way of combining the logistical opportunities created by the consumer who owes no affiliation to either the out-of-town retail parks or to the town centre retailer. In June 1994, the Planning Authorities in Preston gave Tesco the go-ahead to proceed with a top-up retail unit, following Tesco's success in London with such units.

Based upon the survey conducted during 1994 and 1995, looking at town centre and out-of-town shopping habits, a detailed evaluation of Preston as a shopping location is provided. The research findings go some way towards adding a consumer perspective to the ongoing debate surrounding out-of-town retail developments. In the context of Preston, some significant differences in consumer behaviour patterns and perceptions can be shown when comparing those who frequent the town centre with those using out-of-town facilities for their shopping trips. In 1994 the use of the out-of-town location was associated with car travel and less frequent shopping trips, mostly for groceries. Consumers who used the out-of-town shopping facilities were more likely to do most of their shopping in the Preston area. Thus the findings lend some support to Williams' (1992) argument that out-of-town developments prevent leakage of funds from the area. If out-of-town facilities offer overall price advantages to consumers, as asserted by Simmie and Sutcliffe (1994), then this is lost on Preston consumers, who show no awareness of a difference in value for money offered by the two locations.

On the whole, visitors to the out-of-town location were found to be more purposeful in purchasing intent than those engaged in visits to the town centre, which could serve a variety of functions. Thus, the multi-functional nature of the town centre still facilitates greater interaction between different social functions and encourages a diversity of encounters and purposes. This may be an area to capitalize on in the further development of the town centre, leaving consumers to do their purposeful once-a-week grocery shopping out-of-town and at the same time encouraging them back into the town centre to sample the greater range of facilities on offer in an upgraded, user friendly environment.

The Unit for Retail Planning Information (URPI) produces key demographic data for over 200 shopping centres in Great Britain.[11] Information from the 1991 Census of Population is included for trade areas around each centre, and shows the 1991 usually resident population, the population by age categories, numbers of households, households in owner occupation, households in social classes AB & C1, and car ownership. These briefs supersede *Information Brief 87/2*, which was based on the 1981 Census and provided data for the top 100 shopping centres in Great Britain. The shopping centre information is derived from the URPI *UK Shopping Centre Directory Data Set*, which contains information on 1,218 shopping centres in the United Kingdom. These shopping centres are classified to a seven level ranking, reflecting the retail importance of the centre. This ranking was compiled using a combination of factors, including trade area population, multiple representation, market area, 1971 shopping centre turnover and market intelligence.

Healey & Baker have provided an in-depth guide to rental levels for office and industrial property around the world.[12] Included in the Healey & Baker analysis is an international comparison of the cost of occupying business space and an historical overview of rental activity. The report provides a comprehensive survey of rental levels, quoting values as at December 1996 in both US$ per sq. m per year and in local currency per sq. m per year, unless otherwise indicated. The information on rental data relates to top rates for prime property in each country. These figures reflect Healey & Baker's opinion of the prevailing level of rents in the market, in the light of recent transactions and trends in each location.

An earlier report by the Building Services Research and Information Association offers a definition of retail premises and an overview of retail floorspace.[13] There is an analysis of retail outlets that includes the number, type and size of outlet and a consideration of town centre schemes versus out-of-town.

Verdict, the retail analysts, have produced a major report which examines the march of progress of the superstore at the expense of the high street shop.[14] They forecast that by the year 2001 the number of superstores will have grown by another 24.5% to 6,070 and that these will occupy 27.5% of all retail space. Also, by the year 2001, superstores will generate around a third of all retail sales. In 1996 superstores generated 28.7% of total retail sales, double the proportion of a decade ago. Over the next five years, this will increase to 33.7%. The other main conclusions of the report are:-

- in the grocery sector new openings have slowed considerably. Market saturation led to a number of superstore closures in the DIY and electricals sectors in 1996. Growth in numbers is now coming from furniture and carpets superstores with the main players leading a concerted attack on the traditional dominance of the high street.

- planning problems and a lack of suitable sites have combined to put a severe block on much projected development, especially within the 'others' less traditional superstores retail group. Marks and Spencer opened no new out-of-town stores last year while companies trading in areas like office products and sports equipment are facing an uphill battle with planning permission. Clothing retailers in particular will find it difficult to escape planning guidelines designed to preserve high street comparison shopping.

- beyond grocery, DIY, electricals and furniture, which are 'traditional' superstore sectors, are a wide variety of retailers adopting this style of trading, such as Marks & Spencer, Halfords, Toys R Us, Office World plus some trials of comparison high street formats like Burton, River Island, Next and Boots.

- Marks & Spencer dominates the 'other' superstore category with a 39.4% market share. Its share has been eroded over the past five years by much faster physical growth from other retailers such as PetsMart, Office World etc.

- much future out-of-town sales growth will come from the 'other' superstore category as it is less mature than grocery, DIY, electricals or furniture. Many types of retailing could be interested in enjoying the benefits of superstore retailing but expansion is likely to be inhibited by a planning policy which is keen to keep comparison retailers on the high street.

Table 2.2 Store Numbers: Out of Town vs High Street 1987-1996

Year	Superstores	Total Retail Outlets	Superstores As % Of All Outlets
1987	2,355	291,260	0.8
1988	2,718	290,085	0.9
1989	2,995	287,778	1.0
1990	3,232	283,644	1.1
1991	3,361	276,293	1.2
1992	3,584	269,325	1.3
1993	3,850	263,569	1.5
1994	4,169	259,031	1.6
1995	4,527	254,300	1.8
1996	4,877	249,874	2.0

(Source: Verdict Analysis)

The Planning Environment

With successive revisions of planning policy over the past four years, the previous Government committed itself to achieving what has become known as sustainable development. In practical terms this means reducing the overall need to travel and, specifically, discouraging dependence on cars as a means of doing it. The theory that out-of-town stores encourage greater congestion and car usage is debatable. What is not in doubt is the negative impact these policy revisions are having, and will continue to have, on future development.

In June 1996 the previous Government issued a further revision to Planning Policy Guidance 6 concerning town centres and retail developments. This is intended to operate hand-in-hand with transport PPG 13, which attempts to make sure that developments likely to stimulate travel are well served by public transport.

"It is not the role of the planning system," reads the PPG 6 revision, "to restrict competition, preserve existing commercial interests or to prevent innovation." But it explicitly states that out-of-town sites should only be considered if there are no alternatives closer to the town centre, and if the site is "genuinely accessible" by a "choice of means of transport." Developers must demonstrate they have thoroughly assessed all town centre and edge-of-town options first, adopting a "sequential approach" to prospective sites. In addition, they need to weigh carefully the impact on town centre "evening economies" of out-of-town leisure and entertainment outlets like multi-screen cinemas.

PPG 6 does acknowledge that retail warehouse parks 'may' facilitate the selling of bulky goods in large showrooms whereas town centres cannot – in such cases alternative forms of transport apart from the car should be made available. But classic comparison shopping (which by implication means recent high growth areas like sports, toys, pets and fashion) ought to remain the province of the high street, with local authorities expressly advised to "avoid the sporadic siting of comparison shopping out of centres, especially along road corridors."

(This last clause seems specifically designed to scupper further development of new "hybrid" out-of-town sites like Fosse Park in Leicester and Brookfield Park in Cheshunt, where familiar high street retailers trade. The Fort in Birmingham, which opened in March 1997 just off junction 5 of the M6, is almost entirely composed of high street names like River Island, Oasis, Richards and HMV. It carries just one superstore specialist, Shoe City.)

There has been feverish demand for this type of site from both retailers and developers; fewer than a third of the UK's 385 retail parks have no restrictions on the type of tenant they take. For retailers, these locations offer excellent returns. Next at Fosse Park became the company's best performing store within a short time of opening. For developers, rents are as much as 55% higher compared to traditional warehouses where use is restricted to bulky goods only. But PPG6 makes it impossible for high street clothing retailers to formulate an out-of-town strategy because they simply cannot depend on site opportunities. There may be an occasional opportunity, but not necessarily in the high traffic areas companies may want – which in turn will make them less attractive as revenue generators.

As the name suggests, PPGs are guidance, not law. Local authorities are free to interpret them as they wish, and developers are already complaining about a marked lack of consistency in decisions made over the past 12 months. It is clear that there is certainly no blanket ban on developments out-of-town. Their big selling point continues to be the provision of jobs, and in particular their ability to offset a decline in manufacturing jobs. Developers have always been encouraged to strike deals offering additional benefits to the community in exchange for retail expansion, perhaps by building new schools or leisure amenities or providing pump-priming investment as an aid to urban regeneration. Now the bartering – or more accurately, compromising – of refused plans in return for development more suited to local strategies is bound to increase. Already projects more in keeping with the spirit of PPG6 are starting to appear with the opening and improving of more high street shopping centres.

Equally it would be dangerous to rely on flexible local interpretation of national guidelines. The Government has shown itself quite prepared to intervene if it feels the wrong decision has been made at local level. In June 1996 the Department of the Environment quashed plans for a 150,000 square foot factory outlet centre at Tewkesbury in Gloucestershire. Two years earlier Tewkesbury council and a public enquiry had approved the scheme, but the then Environment Secretary John Gummer said the site could not be reached easily by public transport and that the developer, RAM Euro Centers, had failed to consider alternative sites closer to the town centre. Presenting its case cost RAM £200,000 over the two-year enquiry period.

Despite this gloomy outlook, however, a number of sites will continue to pass the PPG tests, particularly given the broadly favourable attitude to new openings for stores selling bulky items. A good example of this opened adjacent to Fosse Park at the end of May 1997 – a 130,000 square foot development with a licence to trade which is limited to bulky goods only (Currys, PC World, DFS) to guard against any further impact on Leicester city centre.

Developers are also sub-dividing existing units (where planning permission allows them to do this) in an effort to push rents up. The former Cargo Club warehouse in Croydon has been converted to seven smaller stores plus a fast-food outlet.

With one eye on the impending clampdown and another on stimulating growth in less saturated superstore markets, there has been a rush over the last two years to ease restrictive planning conditions and seek extensions to existing sites. The emergence of a two-tier market for retail parks in terms of the rents they are able to command was obvious long before the latest revision to PPG6. Property owners would have been well advised to explore user constraints sooner rather than later to secure profitability in emerging new areas. Given that planning consents hold good for five years, there is likely to be a rush to push this last-ditch development through before the turn of the century.

There is still great scope for re-organising and rationalising existing space with developers finding it easier to extend permission for existing sites from restricted to semi-restricted. This will reinforce the development of this two-tier market where mature superstores on semi-restricted sites are driven out by high rents to nearby restricted sites with much lower occupancy costs. This would serve to create ghettos of bulky goods specialists in maturing markets and bring in newer, "better quality" (developers' parlance for higher-paying) tenants. The usual exit costs are unlikely to apply – landlords will be so keen to attract a long term higher-paying tenant they may even be prepared to offer cash incentives to encourage existing tenants to surrender their lease.

As RAM Euro Centers found out, however, the whole process of securing sites out-of-town will be much more time-consuming and expensive. It is this prospect of a long, hard struggle which will discourage the submission of plans in the first place. The bulk of space expansion out-of-town for sectors like food superstores will focus on extension and improvement of existing stores by means of new facilities like chemists, crèches or dry cleaners.

Little has changed since the last Election. After a period of uncertainty and vigorous lobbying from retailers, Labour went on the record as saying that it too wishes to discourage development out-of-town – although there may be particular circumstances, it has emphasised, where some projects will go ahead.

In seeking to limit what has clearly been one of the most successful areas of retailing in recent years, what will prove acceptable under the new planning regime will be a compromise which is far less acceptable not just to retailers but consumers too. Both prefer space, the ability to drive and park plus easily accessible locations. To restrict out-of-town retailing invariably means finding a way to prevent people using their cars. Planning restrictions are as unlikely to do that as they are to revive town centres, which had already started to decline before the advent of superstores.

Verdict concludes that, while superstore development has been severely checked by market saturation and the effect of planning restrictions, the momentum for further growth remains. Electricals and furniture, in particular, are entering a new phase of development, while grocers will continue to improve sales densities by refining product mix and stock management.

The number of new stores will rise by 24% to 6,070 in 2001 and will occupy 26.4% of total retail space compared to 23.8% now. Numerical growth will be more pronounced than physical growth as smaller stores and extensions to existing sites form a larger proportion of new floorspace. It is notable, however, that year-on-year growth in numbers will fall from 7.7% in 1996 to just 2.8% in 2001, due to lack of quality sites and planning refusals.

DIY, the superstore sector most suffering from overcapacity, will show the smallest growth in numbers with just 81 new stores in the entire period. Stores in the "other" category will open most new outlets. Despite opposition from planners they are expected to add another 440 stores within the next five years to bring their total to 1,411. Next will be furniture with 350 new stores, followed by electricals with around 222 and grocers with about 80.

While numbers growth will slow, however, the importance of out-of-town within retailing will remain undiminished. Superstores will account for 32.2% of all retail sales by the year 2001 as against 30.5% in 1996. The best sales performance should be achieved by "other" retailers, closely followed by electricals and then furniture.

According to Verdict, the outlook for the market in terms of sales per square foot is very good. Despite product price deflation and a forecast doubling of footage over the next five years, electricals will see the best growth with sales densities forecast to rise by nearly 44%. Next will come grocers, raising their productivity by 29% to just short of £1160 per sq ft. DIY is a whisker behind, rising by 28.9% on the back of some store rationalisation and consumer demand. Lastly is furniture, whose increase of just 11% will see sales per square foot fall back to £191 after peaking in 1999 at £201.

Even Boots the Chemist, one of the high street's staunchest supporters, has recently joined the exodus out of town.[15] Boots has decided on a complete U-turn in its expansion strategy so that the chemist chain can concentrate future growth on out-of-town developments rather than traditional high streets. Boots, which also owns Halfords and Do-It-All and is now the UK's largest retailer with more than 2,300 branches, had planned to open 70 new Boots the Chemist superstores and 200 new high street outlets. But the group's existing edge-of-town superstores are performing so well it has now ditched that strategy and now plans to open just 70 new high street outlets and up to 200 out-of-town stores.

Average beauty product sales at the out-of-town stores are double their high street levels and the new superstores are not stealing sales from existing high street outlets in the same towns. According to Boots executives, they have become a "browsing" destination for weekend recreational shoppers.

While the Government is resisting new planning applications for out-of-town retail developments, Boots will rarely need planning permission. Unlike supermarkets, Boots the Chemist does not need to have stores built to order, but can convert existing vacant premises. The demise of some out-of-town retailers, like the shoe stores recently shut down or sold off by Sears, has left many suitable premises available. Boots, however, says it remains committed to traditional high streets and will not be abandoning new in-town developments. It is investing more than £25 million updating its London stores.

The chemist chain's decision to head for the outskirts of towns and cities comes as the leading supermarket groups are doing the reverse. After a decade of explosive growth in the number of out-of-town supermarkets, which has left many provincial town centres looking dilapidated and empty, Tesco and Sainsbury's are pouring resources back into town centres. Their move comes as the merged Kwik Save-Somerfield operation promises higher quality high street competition. Boots also has plans to expand other new types of outlet. It is piloting stores inside hospitals and at motorway service stations and airports.

A generation ago, Tesco and Sainsbury's were just shops in the high street. But their metamorphosis from grocers to out-of-town superstores has transfigured the British urban landscape almost beyond recognition.[16] The price of convenience has been an increase in traffic pollution and inadequate nutrition among the inner-city poor. The planners now admit that they got it wrong. Allowing the unchecked march of the supermarkets to new sites on the leafy fringes of Britain's towns and cities created a host of social and environmental problems. "They got planning permission far too easily," said Chris Griffin, of the National Housing and Town Planning Council. "That has been to the detriment of town centres."

For Chris Griffin's predecessors, the planners of the Sixties and Seventies, the problems were far less obvious. Supermarkets offered to build extra roads and expansive car parks to accommodate their customers and cause minimal inconvenience. Some bartered with planning officers by promising to build health or community centres. The result is that today Britain has more than 1,000 superstores, whilst in town shopping centres many stores have been left empty and derelict. Mr Griffin said: "Lots of green fields have gone and some sites of special scientific interest have gone. Then again, a lot of people would say shopping is easier these days."

As the stores have moved out of town, so the shoppers have followed in their cars. In the past 20 years, shopping travel has increased by 300 miles per person per year. The proportion of shopping trips made in the car has increased from 32% to 50% over the same period. Simon Festing, planning campaigner for Friends of the Earth, believes the out-of-town supermarkets have contributed to suburban sprawl and increased car dependency. "The retail trip is one of the fastest rising sectors of traffic growth," he says. Despite the building of access roads, some of the out-of-town supermarkets have created traffic congestion which is now at crisis point. In the Newbury area, where environmental protestors have repeatedly clashed with developers attempting to build a bypass, many locals trace the roots of the problem to the building of two out-of-town supermarkets, whose car-borne customers now clog up the original bypass.

But the supermarkets' colonisation of the green fields has enabled what were once family-run grocery concerns to grow into the blue-chip monoliths which offer the British consumer a quality of service and breadth of choice unparalleled in equivalent stores anywhere else in the world. While the largest high street sites offered only 10,000 square feet of space, the supermarkets – Asda and Tesco especially – have been willing to spend upwards of £20m on building stores up to 40,000 sq ft. David Hughes, professor of agriculture at Wye College, London University, said: "We've got cars. We like to do one-stop shopping and it was impossible to provide that in the centre of town." Lord MacLaurin, chairman of Tesco, is widely credited for first spotting the potential of out-of-town shopping – setting up "Operation Checkout", which transformed the company's financial position.

The scale of operation of the big four – Tesco, Sainsbury's, Asda and Safeway – has enabled them to drive down cost and price. High street stores cannot compete: a generation ago, there were 40,000 independent retailers. Now there are barely 10,000. Grocers are closing at the rate of 800 a year, butchers by over 1,000 a year. Similarly, the number of market traders has halved in the last four years.

Douglas Henderson, chief executive of the Food Produce Consortium, has pointed out that 30% of the population does not have access to cars. "Elderly people and those on low incomes find getting to supermarkets extremely difficult," he says. "We have a growth of people who are becoming nutritionally vulnerable." He added that there were many areas in the country, such as parts of Glasgow, where nutritional food was simply not available. "As a social consequence of the collapse of the independent retailers, people are getting their energy from the fat on chips," he says.

But there are signs that out-of-town shopping may have peaked, new curbs on the building of new superstores are beginning to take effect. Furthermore, says Richard Hyman, chairman of Verdict, out-of-town superstores are at saturation point. "It's the law of diminishing returns. Many people now have access to three or four superstores competing in the same area." In considering planning implications for superstores, Verdict believe "the retail development sector found a fairly implacable foe to out-of-town shopping investment in the previous Secretary for State for the Environment, John Selwyn Gummer. The new Labour administration has been in power since May and developers are, not unnaturally, eager to see if any changes in policy are evident. Under John Prescott's expanded Environment ministry, is Planning Minister Richard Caborn going to be a softer touch?"[17]

At an official level the message is no change. Richard Caborn has stated his desire to continue with John Gummer's policies and to steer development into town centres or edge-of-town locations. Many commentators seized upon the decision in July 1997 to grant Sainsbury's consent for a new superstore in Richmond as evidence of a policy change. Press innuendoes even suggested that this decision was linked to the political donation Lord Sainsbury had made to the Labour Party. Closer examination has shown that policy has not changed. Firstly, Richmond was an independent public inquiry inspector's decision, not the Secretary of State's. Sainsbury's successfully demonstrated need in the catchment area and jumped over the sequential test/transport hurdles because no sites for a superstore exist in, or adjacent to, Richmond town centre. With this site, Sainsbury's played by the rules and won fairly, despite local opposition. Things have certainly not gone all Sainsbury's way and it has actually had four refusals including two retail park developments. Strict interpretation of PPG6 and PPG13 guidelines are still very evident.

Safeway has had a much better run with four approvals out of four under its belt. This success rate is down to good schemes that have been well argued – going with rather than against planning policy. Safeway's approval at Bath successfully used transport arguments to prove need. The site is in the east of the city – an area poorly served by existing superstores to the west. Traffic congestion is so bad in Bath city centre (and its geography does funnel all traffic into or through the centre) that many food shoppers found it easier to travel some distance to neighbouring towns such as Chippenham or Trowbridge. The new Safeway will satisfy this need in East Bath and cut down on out of centre car journeys by local shoppers. At Woking Safeway won out against Tesco despite the latter being originally backed by the Local Authority. The need for a superstore was not disputed. Tesco won permission first and hence the Local Authority felt bound to reject Safeway. These decisions were reversed on appeal by the Secretary of State because Safeway's scheme was nearer to the town centre and hence better satisfied the PPG6 criteria.

Recent years have seen a number of important changes affecting retail planning. Against a growing background of concern that town centres were not being revitalised, planning policy changes aim to refocus investment back onto the high street. These changes can be summed up by the rise of the sequential test, the requirement for non-vehicular access to new stores, along with greater concern about the quality of new shops' design.

The new framework has been articulated in three Planning Policy Guidance notes covering general planning principles (PPG1), town centres and retail development (PPG6) and transport and accessibility (PPG13). These policy changes aim to channel retail development into where local politicians and planners deem that it will have the most overall benefit to the whole community – the existing high street. The sequential test, introduced in PPG6, aims to restrict permission for out-of-town stores only where suitable town centre or edge of centre sites are not available. The onus has been placed on the developer to prove that this is the case.

In addition, the transport series of PPG13 also require the accessibility of non-car users to be assessed. This covers not just whether the less mobile can get to an out-of-town store, but also whether such a new development would affect the viability of a more non-car accessible outlet located elsewhere (usually in a neighbouring town centre). The effect of an out-of-town development on overall shopping patterns and frequency/length of car journeys, has also to be considered.

The tests required by the planning process represent a number of stiff hurdles that need to be cleared before permission to develop is granted. Developers and retailers need to be far more pro-active in arguing their case to local authorities and this acts to slow down and raise the cost of the new store development process.

Most recent decisions on superstore planning applications started life under the previous government. The various Planning Policy Guidance notes and their interpretation by politicians and planners, are at least shaking up into some sort of a pattern. It is not easier to win planning permission for out-of-town superstores, but the rules of the game are now better understood. Retailers and developers realise that they have got to try harder to persuade Local Authorities to grant them planning permission and to be creative in marshalling their arguments.

Using consumer research, Tesco have argued that a network of well planned out-of-town stores that are easily accessible, will lead to less car use than today's existing and poorly planned provision in the high street. At present their arguments have fallen on deaf ears. It remains to be seen whether a Labour Government is more receptive, with a view to cutting car use and helping to meet the pollution reducing targets agreed at the Kyoto summit.

There have been a number of studies in recent years that have analysed the space requirements for shopping centre service areas. One such study was commissioned in 1994 by the British Council of Shopping Centres, and was carried out on their behalf by consultants Symonds Travers Morgan.[18] The surveys were specifically aimed at medium-sized shopping centres in town centre locations, rather than out-of-town. It is in such locations that restricted site areas and highway infrastructure place greater emphasis on the need for efficient service area planning. An important aspect of this study was the range of management systems and measures that were observed. Many measures can be taken that are within the jurisdiction of the shopping centre manager and which will serve to improve operations in the delivery yard and loading bay. These include access control measures such as entrance barriers, restriction on parking time, ensuring shop staff are informed of imminent deliveries, vehicle access records, effective signage, co-ordination between store and centre management, regular yard patrols and, as a last resort, clamping for persistent offenders.

The results of this study suggested that there is scope for reducing the size of servicing areas in shopping centres, as compared with the level of provision typically adopted hitherto. It was recommended that the data supplied by the survey be reviewed periodically, to take account of changing delivery patterns, seven-day trading and similar developments in the industry. The results of this study by Mynors and Rose should be of benefit both to the transport profession and the retail industry.

Change has been a widespread and sometimes dramatic feature of the retail environment of British cities in recent years. New facilities ranging from superstores through retail warehouses and retail parks to regional shopping centres have been added to the retail scene. Inevitably, these have had negative impacts on some of the traditional shopping centres at all hierarchical levels. An article by Thomas and Bromley has examined the plight of the less-advantageously located district shopping centres by focusing on a particular case study in South Wales.[19] The circumstances associated with the development of a 'spiral of retail decline' in such centres are examined, and the potential for commercial revitalisation is evaluated. Public intervention appears essential to initiate a process of regeneration. Without such action, the future of many small shopping centres is likely to be weak and bleak, and the local shopping opportunities available to the less mobile elements of the community will continue to decline.

The eighth edition of the multi-volume work *Retail Trade International*, from market research publisher Euromonitor, provides an overview of retailing in countries around the world. The section on the United Kingdom discusses the issue of town centre versus out-of-town retailing. According to Euromonitor, the increase in demand for one-stop shopping has fuelled the rise in indoor shopping centres. Their figures indicate that, at the end of 1992, there were 950 shopping centres (as opposed to high streets) in the UK, 43% constituting out-of-town sites, of which 58% were retail parks. Out-of-town activity peaked in the boom of the mid-1980s, slowing rapidly at the tail end of the decade as soon as consumer spending showed signs of slowing. However, the building of retail parks gained pace in 1990, and was the preferred option for most expansion throughout the decade. Research surveys have revealed that over half of enclosed shopping centre occupiers are dissatisfied with their location, stemming from concern over occupancy costs, especially service charges, poor/restrictive management and inflexible opening hours.

As parks have risen in popularity with retailers, especially food retailers, so sites have become larger and more comprehensive and aesthetically pleasing. Complementary big-shed operators and smaller specialist shops are increasingly grouping together at the conception stage rather than on an ad hoc basis. New site development quickened as the UK edged out of recession and foreign operators broke into the market. With respect to mixed retailing, Marks & Spencer and John Lewis were amongst the earliest to invest in out-of-town development, whilst others, such as Boots, have been slower to take up the cudgel.

Out-of-town sites did not suffer to the same extent as the high street during the recession, with economising consumers prepared to travel further afield to get a bargain. The higher level of service – ease of access, longer opening hours, and better facilities – has continued to draw custom away from congested town centres. Public concern over the disregard of green belts, playing fields and wildlife led to the review of planning regulations which has seen the clamp down on new out-of-town developments. The concern, of course, is that this move will not necessarily breathe life back into the high street. For example, the conversion of redundant business parks is a plausible alternative. As Euromonitor observe, an estimated 30 retail parks were opened during 1993; a further 120 sites were in various stages of completion, whilst at least another 70 planning applications were being processed at the time their report was produced.

Also in *Retail Trade International*, Euromonitor consider other key areas such as credit cards, teleshopping and concessions. They believe home shopping is the most likely sector through which the so-called 'Euro-consumer' may materialise. Mail order companies' prices differ from country to country and the home shopper could potentially benefit from shopping around. However, it is likely that customers will foresee problems with pan-European mail order, such as not being able to return or exchange faulty goods. For this reason, the European Commission sees the need for consumer protection legislation to encourage pan-European shopping.

The *Goad Out of Town Centre Shopping Directory* provides details of retail operations of over 10,000 square feet.[21] All the entries fall outside of major town shopping centres and therefore do not appear on the *UK Shopping Centre Plans* published by Charles Goad (who have produced maps and plans since 1875). The information used to compile the directory is derived from a variety of sources: field research by surveyors, press cuttings, retailers' branch listings, Company Reports and information supplied by local authority planning departments concerning proposed or consented developments. All the information for the directory is derived from the Goad Out of Centre Shopping Database. This provides wider coverage of smaller outlets and greater detail on each recorded location than is available in the directory. As this database is being constantly updated it serves to offer a current view of out of centre shopping.

For each outlet listed in the directory details are given of the retailer's trading fascia, a description of the retailer's trade, gross and/or net square footage, number of parking spaces and Ordnance Survey National Grid Reference. Details are also given for planned locations. These are developments planned, consented, under construction, under inquiry etc. For these entries details include the developer's name, agent's name and planning status/proposed trade development. The easy to use layout (by geographical area) makes the directory an indispensble reference tool.

Goad also produce Shopping Centre Plans and Bespoke Shopping Centre Plans; Retail Geographic Information System and Derived Databases; a Phone-In Retail Report Bureau Service; Out of Centre Shopping Information; Pedestrian Flowcount Reports; and Demographic Reports. These services provided by Goad will be of increasing value to retail planners; especially as local authorities are at last being given the powers needed to contain the move out-of-town by retailers seen during the late 1980s and early 1990s.

References

1   Hayward R and McGlynn S, The Town Centres We Deserve?: Guidance for Planning, Design and Management: a Review Article, *Town Planning Review*, 66 (3), 1995.

2   ibid.

3   Royal Institution of Chartered Surveyors, Planning Policy Guidance Note 6 (Revised): Town Centres and Retail Development: Comments by RICS, 1995.

4   Revitalising London's Town Centres : a Vision for London report and the proceedings of the 1995 Vision for London Symposium and Workshop on Town Centres – London, 1996.

5   Smulian M, All Roads Lead to Bluewater, *Surveyor*, 23 January 1997, 18-20.

6   Store Wars, *Guardian*, 9/9/98.

7   *Shopping Centres in the Pipeline*, May/October 1997, London: Hillier Parker.

8   Alzubaidi, H., Vignali, C., Davies, B.J., Schmidt, R.A., Town centre versus out-of-town shopping: a consumer perspective, *International Journal of Retail & Distribution Management*, Vol.25, no.2, 1997, pp.78-89.

9   MacDonald, G. (1987), "How the out of town shops help the centre", *Town and Country Planning*, February, pp.46-7.

10 Thomas, C.J. and Bromley, R.D.F. (1993), "The impact of out-of-centre retailing", in Bromley, R.D.F. and Thomas, C.J. (Eds), *Retail Change, Contemporary Issues*, UCL Press, London.

11 Unit for Retail Planning Information, Key Demographics for Shopping Centres in GB, *Information Brief* 6/94 etc.

12 Healey & Baker, *Business Space Across the World*, London, 1997.

13 Samuelsson-Brown, G. and Whittome, S. (1992) *The Retail Sector: a Review of Floorspace, Building Type, Market Potential and Construction Activity, Great Britain*, Building Services Research and Information Association, Bracknell, 1992.

14 Verdict, *Out-of-Town vs the High Street*, London, 1997.

15 Boots U-turns out of town: retailer goes against the trend, *Guardian*, 30/3/98.

16 Britain's new barons battle for shopping supremacy, *Independent*, 29/12/97.

17 Planning for superstores, *Retail Verdict UK*, December 1997, p8–10.

18 Mynors P and Rose T, Servicing areas for shopping centres, *Traffic Engineering and Control*, January 1996 p19–25.

19 Thomas C and Bromley R, Retail decline and the opportunities for commercial revitalisation of small shopping centres: a case study in South Wales, *Town Planning Review*, 66 (4), 1995.

20 Euromonitor, *Retail Trade International*, London, 1995.

21 Charles Goad Ltd, *Goad Out of Centre Shopping Directory*, Old Hatfield, annual.

3   Open All Hours at the One-Stop Shop

Tesco is pressing on towards the "24-hour society" with 63 of its 588 stores now trading around the clock.[1] The stores open from Monday morning to Saturday night, closing only for the hours on Sunday required by law. More than 20 million people are now just a short drive away from an open checkout in the middle of the night. Terry Leahy, the group's chief executive, said the chain was responding to Britain's changing lifestyles. He cited a report from the Future Foundation which disclosed that growing numbers of people work through the night and want to shop during these "unsocial" hours. The report suggested five million shoppers want grocery stores to stay open all night, while a million people are working regularly until 11pm. More than 300,000 people are now at work between 2am and 5am, and these numbers are expected to double over the next ten years.

Tesco is well ahead of its rivals, with only Asda currently interested in all-night shopping beyond Friday. A spokesman admitted that shopping activity in the middle of the night was relatively low, even by the standards of a quiet weekday morning. Shopping tends to drop off after 1am, picking up again after four in the morning. But he pointed out that most large stores are staffed around the clock with cleaners, security and shelf-filling activity, and said such staff welcomed the opportunity to meet customers. Midnight shopping is naturally popular with shift workers, but Tesco has also observed other categories of customer. They include parents of young children who take the opportunity to shop without dragging screaming babies around the store. Trolleys tend to fill with the same mix of products as during the day, except for alcohol, which cannot be sold out of licensed hours.

One of the most important works to discuss the social issues inherent in retailing appeared in 1996 as an Institute of Economic Affairs *Hobart Paper*. Burke and Shackleton look at trends in retailing, competition in retailing, regulatory and environmental issues, the contribution of retailing and public policy conclusions. Amongst other questions, they ask whether there should be curbs on out-of-town and edge-of-town shopping because of its effect on town centres and on the areas where big stores are now being located. For example, should opening hours be regulated? Is there something 'inferior' about employment in retailing as compared with employment in manufacturing? Burke and Shackleton of the University of

Westminster take up the challenge of addressing these key questions about British retailing. They conclude that "... concerns about the overall market structure in UK retailing are exaggerated: although there is a fairly small number of big players with large market shares, there is a high degree of competition from both traditional and new forms of retailing."[2]

As for regulation, Burke and Shackleton argue for 'complete deregulation of opening hours' and see no need for more consumer protection regulation: competition among retailers to maintain high product quality standards is more effective than government mandates. On the 'central policy question of the moment' – using the planning process to restrict out-of-town and edge-of-town developments – Burke and Shackleton oppose regulation which, they claim, will benefit retailers already located in such areas and larger groups generally, as well as going against consumers' revealed preferences. Environmental considerations are important, but they should apply not only to large retailers; in any case, the environmental consequences of regulating location may be adverse. The authors' general conclusion is that retailing "... is an efficient and innovative industry which is of great direct and indirect importance to the UK economy; the costs of interfering with its development, or trying to reverse it, are likely to exceed the benefits."[3]

Burke and Shackleton highlight a number of growing concerns:

- that the move towards out-of-town retailing increases the use of cars (and thus pollution and other external costs)
- that it eats up valuable greenfield locations
- that it leads to declining and increasingly run-down city centres
- that the purchasing power of large supermarkets penalises small food producers
- leads (allegedly) to distorted agricultural systems in Third World countries.

Current retailing trends, particularly the move towards out-of-town sites, are also claimed to penalise older, poorer and less mobile members of the population by reducing their choices and increasing their shopping and travel costs. Burke and Shackleton survey a range of actual or potential public policy issues which arise in retailing, within the context of an overview of the changing nature of the sector, and critically assess the case for renewed government intervention.

The evidence presented by Burke and Shackleton points to UK retailing being both dynamic and competitive, despite a relatively high degree of concentration. It is dynamic in the sense that new forms of retailing are constantly emerging, as old forms shrink or whither away; it is competitive in that barriers to entry are low, consumers are offered a choice of retailing bundles (price, range, quality, access, convenience, ambience), and the less successful retailers are subject to exit, regardless of the scale of their operation. It is felt that concerns about the overall market structure in UK retailing are exaggerated: although there is a fairly small number of big players with large market shares, there is a high degree of competition from both traditional and new forms of retailing. Similarly, Burke and Shackleton do not agree that further regulation of retail location and opening hours is required. Indeed, they argue for significant deregulation in some areas. In particular, they are opposed to using regulatory powers to prevent the drift of certain types of retailing to out-of-town sites. If people clearly want to shop for bulky and heavy items in more convenient locations than the traditional high street, they should be enabled to do so wherever possible.

The central policy question of the moment concerns the use of the planning process to limit out-of-town or edge-of-town development to situations where the would-be retailer is able to prove that the new superstore will have no impact on local shopping centres. Such a rule favours the existing edge-of-town retailers (who in some cases face almost saturated markets and are therefore only too happy to see competition excluded) and the larger multiple retailers who, unlike their smaller competitors, have the resources to hire the necessary experts to challenge planning decisions. In conclusion, Burke and Shakleton argue against significant further regulation of retailing. They reiterate that this is an efficient and innovative industry which is of great direct and indirect importance to the UK economy; the costs of interfering with its development, or trying to reverse it, are likely to exceed the benefits.

Retail commentator Edward Hammond would not have won many prizes for trend-spotting in the ferocious world of the modern supermarket. When, in 1951, Hammond dismissed the US self-service store in the British shopkeepers' bible, the *Modern Grocer and Provision Merchant*, as a "class of emporium unlikely to ever come to this country", he was already three years behind the times. Far from customers proving culturally allergic to do-it-yourself shopping, its overnight popularity heralded a revolution that changed for ever the way we shop.

Self-service rapidly began to replace traditional, counter-based stores, but it was the end of rationing and the easing of building restrictions that allowed supermarkets to flourish. In 1956, the newly-won freedom to set food prices further fuelled the pace of change by spurring price wars. From the 1970s, competition between stores moved into the realms of technology, shop design, a wider range of groceries – including 'ethnic' and convenience foods – and longer opening hours. To fight on these fronts, the supermarkets needed space, and the out-of-town superstore was born. Shopping had once again moved into a new era.

With free roam of the countryside, the four superchains that dominate the pack – Tesco, Sainsbury's, Asda and Safeway – came of age in the 1980s. The superchains evolved into vastly efficient, slick marketing machines of world-class proportions. The war had entered a new dimension, with fewer combatants but renewed impetus and higher stakes. "As business operations, British supermarkets are the best in the world in terms of efficiency, quality control and the standard of design in stores," claims Dr Ross Davies, director of the Oxford Institute of Retail Management. And David Hughes, professor of marketing at Wye College, University of London, enthuses: "We're not just a nation of shopkeepers, we're a nation of bloody good shopkeepers."

But the glory days when shoppers were easily wooed by coffee shops, cheap petrol, loyalty cards and crèches are over. A more discerning customer, coupled with a static demand for food, a saturated market in terms of store numbers and new planning restrictions, changes the nature of the game. Where store groups have traditionally built their way out of a hole, they are now being forced to look elsewhere for their next buck. "Supermarkets are having to search long and hard for ways of increasing their profitability," explains Paul Rickard, of consumer analysts Mintel. "The biggest problem is that planning restrictions mean they can no longer just plonk new stores down. They are having to make their existing space work a lot harder by extending the products they sell and moving into higher margin areas."

Although supermarkets continue to make ground at the expense of small and specialist retailers – for example, butchers have lost nearly a third of their trade and greengrocers a quarter in the last seven years – it is not enough to ensure future prosperity. Cornering developing markets – for instance, in convenience and take-away food – is paramount. Asda now claims to be the biggest Indian take-away in the country, and it can't be long before home delivery à la Pizza Hut is on the way.

The superchains are racing to provide the ultimate one-stop shopping experience. Beyond the food aisles, moves into fashion, dry-cleaning, opticians, dental surgeries, pharmacies and the rest are symptomatic of the obsession with providing the ultimate selection under one roof. But the 'one-stop shop' is only half the picture. The superchains are hungry for the convenience end of the market. Via the petrol forecourt and a return to the high street, they are fighting for the top-up, secondary shop, putting the independents in the most perilous position since the pilgrimage out-of-town began.

But will it be enough? Professor Hughes thinks not. "The power of supermarkets as we know it will peak this decade," he predicts. "Drudge shopping, for things such as toilet rolls, is not sustainable. People hate it." He believes the future lies in two directions: hi-tech home shopping for necessities, and hi-touch leisure shopping for higher value products with which people expect a certain level of service. "Hi-touch is where we relate to the people who provide the food in store," he explains. "It's that one meal in a week we want to buy from people who know what they're selling. It will be a hobby, something we enjoy doing."

"The reliance we place on a supermarket can transfer to an enormous number of areas," says Dr Richard Elliott, reader in marketing at Oxford University's Said Business School. "The thing that gives supermarkets such powerful brands is the amount of time we spend in them. If we spent as much as much time in a bank or anywhere else, if they treated us reasonably well, we would trust those brands at the same level we trust supermarkets." The superchains' venture into banking – albeit limited, to date – is proof of the power of brand loyalty. With a burgeoning interest in long-term financial security, the store groups are keen to extend their offer to PEPS, pensions and life assurance.

There have already been experiments with estate agencies and travel, and further links with the leisure industry, overseas expansion and car sales are expected. Stores are eagerly anticipating the full deregulation of electricity and water services, and consumer research demonstrates a high level of interest in supermarkets as utility providers. The onset of micro-marketing, using information from loyalty cards, will enable stores to pinpoint individuals and households with specific needs and tailor services accordingly. But is there a limit to what only a handful of companies can sell us? The big four already control more than half the nation's grocery bill. So how far can brand loyalty be pushed? "After a while, brand extension stretches the credibility of your core customer," Professor Hughes suggests. "Eventually, you start to rub away at the edges and your core relationship with your customer starts to disintegrate." Supermarkets take heed. The increasingly wealthy but time-starved customer – the marketing department's dream commodity – is also increasingly discerning about how and where they spend their cash. It's a competitive occupation.

Safeway was a great British buyout, which soared in sales after freeing itself from its huge American parent a decade ago. But it is now under pressure from rivals as it tries to define itself as the supermarket chain for families. At the height of the recession, when supermarkets were floundering, Colin Smith, Chief Executive, set about a massive overhaul of the group, dubbed Safeway 2000. The company refocused and stores now appeal to value-seeking family shoppers rather than to higher-income couples. In this way the number of shoppers increased by 50% in two years, although towards the end of 1997 the group warned of non-existent sales growth, with analysts observing that it was losing out to Sainsbury's.

Smith uses information gleaned by institutions such as the Henley Centre in order to determine Safeway's direction. According to customer development director Roger Partington, the results are often surprising. "We had thought that the shopper just wanted a continuing array of choice and variety, which they do, but it also creates confusion ... Our average supermarkets sell between 22 and 25,000 lines. It can be a bit daunting. So we set about ways to make it easier." It was information from customers that was the genesis of a pilot scheme in Basingstoke, "collect and go", where customers can ring up and order basic grocery items, and collect them when they do their fresh goods shop.

According to one Safeway insider, everything the company does is to make things easier for families. "Harry and Molly [the children in TV advertising] convey our general market position, very much aimed at families with children 0-5," he said. Safeway is also adopting the 'market-hall' concept favoured by Asda, with increasing in-store pharmacies, dry cleaners and own-range kids clothes, replicating the traditional high street. The group thinks there is little left to be gained from straightforward price competition, because the market is now so keen. Safeway has launched "Price Protected" – if customers buy a product cheaper elsewhere, the store gives it to them free. So where next? Last year it launched a venture with BP to base "proper" supermarkets in 24-hour petrol stations. This may not appeal to some but, according to Safeway, it is the future. It must hope so. Because another version of the future in the trade has it that Safeway will be swallowed up by its aggressive, expansionist rival, Asda.

After home shopping, prepare for office shopping. Somerfield has launched a pilot scheme to allow customers to do their shopping from work. The 2,500 staff at the IBM development laboratories in Hursley, Hampshire, are able to place orders via their personal computers, choosing any of the 20,000 products stocked by the local Somerfield store. Somerfield staff collect the goods and then bring them to the IBM car park for delivery, charging a £2 fee. If it succeeds, Somerfield intend to roll out the idea to other big companies. "Our target areas will be the larger offices out of town, with big car parks and where there is no supermarket nearby," said Dave Nevitt, business development analyst at Somerfield. "We have tried to keep the time it takes to fill out an order to the absolute minimum. We are targeting 10 minutes from start to finish," said Nevitt. Other supermarket chains have introduced home-delivery services, with orders coming in either by fax or computer link-up. Somerfield will guage the extra cost of the service, along with its popularity, over a six-month trial period.

Concerns are growing in the banking industry that the decision by the high street banks to form joint ventures with the supermarket groups could be allowing a Trojan Horse into the sector. According to research by Kleinwort Benson, the supermarkets are likely to dump their banking partners if their schemes become successful, choosing to operate the services themselves instead. Banks such as NatWest, Abbey National and Bank of Scotland, which have signed joint ventures with Tesco, Safeway and Sainsbury's respectively, could find that they have provided support for a powerful new group of competitors that could destabilise the sector by exerting pricing pressure. Their report adds that the introduction of well-branded new entrants could be dangerous, given the relatively weak brand names of the high street banks.

Kleinwort's Simon Samuels, who wrote the report, says: "Long-term these supermarket link-ups are bad news for the banking industry. It is quite likely that the supermarkets will choose to go it alone if the idea works. All the banks will have gained is a fee for running the accounts." The mechanism for supermarkets to oust the banks from their partnerships is already in place in some cases. A little known clause in Sainsbury's contract with the Bank of Scotland enables the supermarket group forcibly to buy out the bank's stake after a certain period. The report expressed concerns over NatWest's deal with Tesco as "it gives a new competitor a relatively easy entry into banking."

The fierce battle for supermarket customers has entered a new phase with the decision of Sainsbury's to open 244 information outlets of its planned nationwide bank. Sainsbury's Bank, a joint venture between the supermarket chain and the Bank of Scotland, will operate from Edinburgh as a 24-hour free telephone banking service. Shoppers can get information leaflets from Sainsbury's stores for the scheme which will eventually be extended to all 600 stores. The move is part of Sainsbury's strategy to re-establish itself as the UK's leading supermarket chain, a position it has lost to arch-rival Tesco. It is also further evidence of the growing competition within the UK's financial services industry, especially banking, where the traditional high street clearers are being challenged by new entrants such as insurers, building societies, supermarkets and other retailers.

The first Sainsbury's Bank information booths were opened in Scotland, the North of England and the Midlands. The services available include classic and gold credit cards and two savings accounts – an instant account offering a gross annual interest rate of 5.75% and a Christmas Saver account. Other products, including personal loans, mortgages and insurance are expected to follow. The bank is the first attempt by a supermarket to offer a full telephone banking service. But it is not the first foray into financial services: Tesco has linked up with the Royal Bank of Scotland, having originally been linked to NatWest; Safeway has joined forces with Abbey National; and Barclays has just opened a pilot in-store branch at a Morrisons supermarket.

Sainsbury's is hoping its new bank, in which it has a 55% stake, will boost its Reward loyalty card scheme. Incentives are offered to cardholders who transfer their balances from existing credit and store cards. Points are awarded for using the Sainsbury's credit cards in rival supermarkets. Shoppers can get cash under the existing cashback scheme at the tills as well as from 10,000 Link automated teller machines around the UK. Eventually cash machines will be installed in Sainsbury's stores.

North America holds an endless fascination for the UK development industry and is credited with sparking many of its best retail ideas. Some, such as the covered mall, have endured and some such as the speciality shopping centre, have not. But win or lose, most developers in the UK have an unshakeable belief that US retail concepts will succeed over here. As Paul Sherman reports, "the rapid growth of power retailing is probably the most striking change on the American retail scene."[4] Power centres are a very distant relative to British retail parks and some of the retailers are known to the British shopper. The chief distinction is retail mix and the fact that schemes are built to a much higher specification than in the UK. More than just steel sheds, power centres in the south-west are built to a higher standard than the rest of the US and many developments sport a very distinctive style. Typically, the retail units are clustered in groups around a massive central car park, ensuring that the power centres make their mark on the landscape. Much more important than factory-outlet retailing, this sector has transformed the retail map in the US. Whether you restrict the definition to include only those competing within a single market sector (e.g. Circuit City, which supplies electrical goods) or more general and off-price retailers (Marshalls, TK Maxx, Target and Wal-Mart) they are giving the malls a run for their money.

The fact that conventional malls are now on the defensive is an important consideration for developers and investors outside America who are inspired by this vision of power retailing. The threat posed by the power centres to traditional shopping malls seems very real in the south-west of the US, and in many respects is analogous to the position which many traditional UK town centres find themselves in. Many US consumers have made shopping their second career. A new stratum of choice has been opened up within a retailing environment that already offers more than the British consumer could ever dream of. Which poses the question of whether British retailers could rise to the challenge of providing power centres. Even if planning obstacles could be overcome, that day seems a long way off.

Harold Couch, chairman of the International Council of Shopping Centers – Europe (ICSC), has examined activity in the European shopping centre industry and provided an overview of the range of centres that opened during 1995.[5] Couch's review contains extracts from a speech he delivered at the 1996 ICSC European Conference held in Montreux, Switzerland. Some of the shopping centres discussed are the 20,000m^2 Vilafranca Centro in Vila Franca De Xira, Portugal; the Ski Storsenter in Ski, Norway, a two-level centre covering 25,000m^2; the Nørrebro Bycenter located in the suburbs of Copenhagen, Denmark, with 9,900m^2 of retail space plus 4,100m^2 of office space; and the Pazo de la Maza situated in the medieval town of Lugo in Galencia, Spain, where the 2,500m^2 shopping centre has been adapted from a 17th century palace. These shopping centres are situated either in small towns or within the central business district of large towns. Couch also considers centres described as semi-urban, which are located within the urban area of towns and cities. These include the 22,000m^2 Carousel Shopping Centre in the suburbs of Istanbul in Turkey; the Linden Centre in the former east Berlin has 28,000m^2 of retail space and 3,600m^2 devoted to leisure facilities; the I Portali centre in Modena, Italy which covers 22,300m^2. Examples of suburban shopping centres include the Paunsdorf Centre (111,000m^2) in Leipzig, Germany; the El Ferial centre (24,000m^2) in Madrid, Spain; and the Itaca centre (18,200m^2) in Formia, Italy.

Couch discusses the development of factory outlet malls, which have been an established feature of US shopping centres for many years but are relatively new in Europe. There are signs that this form of non-central or out-of-town development will spread to many parts of Europe during the next five to ten years. He concludes by stating that very high standards have been achieved in the shopping centres that opened in the late 1980s and early 1990s. Consumers now take quality for granted and a centre has to be exceptional in order to attract attention. The greatest potential for new centres continues to be in southern and eastern European countries. Spain, Portugal, Italy and Turkey have considerable potential but the extent of new shopping centre development has slowed because of the effects of recession. However, it is considered likely that the pace of development throughout Europe will increase towards the end of the century.

Twenty-five years after the first franchise in the UK was set up, the idea is undergoing something of a resurgence. Business format franchises accounted for some 3.7% of retail sales in the UK in 1995, up from 3.6% the year before. However, there is still some ground to be made up on the United States, where franchising accounts for 12% of retail sales. In the UK at the end of 1995 there were 474 business format franchises, employing 222,700 people and with sales worth £5.9 billion. Research by management consultants Andersen Consulting and from FT Management Reports' analysis, estimates that 1996 sales from business format franchised outlets will reach:

- $510 billion worldwide
- $287 billion in the US
- $100 billion in the EU

A report by Phillips reviews the main operational issues encountered by franchised retail and service networks, and aims to identify some of the levers by which to secure competitive advantage.[6] It looks at how successful franchise operations such as Seven-Eleven Japan introduced sophisticated supply chain and information technology solutions to secure competitive advantage: and investigates the importance of market research; effective branding and marketing; and well-defined franchisor systems and strong franchisor support.

In order to obtain a quick snapshot of the *British Shopper* it is worth referring to the pocket book of the same name. Produced by NTC, in conjunction with ACNeilsen, it contains essential facts and figures for marketers, advertisers, retailers and manufacturers.[7] It looks at consumer markets, spending patterns and shopping patterns – what, where, when and how the shopper buys. The data includes detailed trends and profiles taken straight from ACNeilsen's comprehensive retail and consumer databases to provide a detailed and up-to-date picture of developments in shopping and retail markets. NTC's guide provides evidence of the important trends in retailing.

Another useful annual publication is produced by the retail trade body, the British Retail Consortium.[8] In it's *Annual Review*, BRC looks at the year's events in the retail trade. The 1996 edition, for example, has sections on consumer issues, food and drink, economic affairs, financial services, operational resources, personnel policy and security and loss prevention. The BRC (the 'Voice of British Retailing') also produces a regular *Retail Crime Costs Survey*, which has helped raise public awareness of the issue of retail crime and encourgaged concerted action.

Whilst the main thrust of this literature review is the threat to the high street retailer by the growth of the out-of-town superstore, it is worth remembering that there are other, less obvious, contenders for the consumers' hard-earned cash. As an example, airport retailing is currently growing faster than high street retailing. Airports around the world are rapidly expanding their retail operations and luring traditional high street retailers to their terminals. In 1994 the world's airport retailing market was worth $12.6 billion. It is predicted to grow by around 60% to reach $20 billion by the year 2000. Gavin Humphries has examined the global issues determining the size and shape of the airport retailing sector.[9] He also considers the various new ventures such as airport entertainment and non-airport retailing that traditional airport operators and retailers have recently established, and concludes with a qualitative analysis defining a successful airport retailer.

Retail groups are increasingly becoming international operations. A number of European retailers can claim to be international, including Carrefour (France), Makro (Netherlands), Delhaize le Lion (Belgium), Royal Ahold (Netherlands), Tengelmann (Germany) and Otto Versand (Germany). Others, notably in the food sector, have only recently begun the internationalisation process. UK retailer Tesco's first international move was in 1992 with the acquisition of Catteau in France, whilst Rewe has only recently moved outside the German market with its acquisition of Billa. Retailers who have traditionally remained within their national borders or who have failed in their previous internationalisation attempts, for example Boots, are now taking a fresh look at international opportunities. Casino, the French retailer, is amongst those European retailers who have confined their overseas ventures to a limited number of countries but who are now becoming more adventurous in their expansion plans.

Lamey has noted that pan-European expansion plans are being assisted by the major advances in telecommunications.[10] Cross-border retail operations and the increasing significance of non-store retail channels are underpinned by an increasingly sophisticated European telecommunications infrastructure based on digital exchanges and fibre optic cable. The cost of call-centre technology has come down and consultants Ovum forecast in their report *Computer Telephone Integration: the Business Opportunity* that the CTI market in Europe will grow from £336.8 million in 1995 to over £2 billion in 2000.

The United States continues to exert an influence over European retail as many US companies have begun to target Europe. In the European market, US companies are seen to have three advantages over local retailers: higher levels of customer service; more innovative store designs; and more sophisticated technology. Also, many of the retail initiatives currently sweeping Europe, including Efficient Customer Response (ECR) and Category Management originated in the US. The UK is seen as a natural stepping stone for North American retailers. There are no language barriers and there are opportunities to offer customers something different as well as high levels of customer service.

Lamey provides an insight into the pan-European expansion strategies being pursued by large non-European retail operators. The companies studied include Nike, exploiting the European market with three different formats; La Senza, with a strong customer services element; Red Earth, the Australian competitor of the Body Shop; and Talbots, using mail order to raise awareness of the company's brand.

In the UK, the best general overview is provided by the consumer market research publisher Key Note.[11] This report offers a relatively up-to-date analysis of the retail trade in the UK. There is a useful section which considers the factors influencing retailing in the economy as a whole. Key Note believes the future prospects for UK retailing are inextricably linked to the trends taking place within the larger retailers; forecasts of consumer confidence, expenditure, savings and disposable incomes; the state of the housing market; and the fortunes and philosophy of the Government of the day.

Within large retailers, a number of trends are apparent. The expanding use of customer loyalty systems, which started in food, but is now spreading to other forms of retailing, is improving the communications between retailers and their customers and providing a solid base of information on consumer purchasing habits. Further developments are likely to lead to improved targeted marketing and new customer services. One significant new development stemming from loyalty cards is the launch into personal banking and other financial services by a number of the largest food retailers.

The largest food retailers are becoming starved of development potential. The changes to local planning guidelines issued by government has restricted the number of out-of-town large store developments. To satisfy the demands of shareholders, they must now look elsewhere for profits growth. Overseas development is an obvious option; another is to increase the number of non-food departments within their large stores; and yet another is to acquire other non-food retail businesses in order to gain prime sites e.g. Littlewoods.

Key Note forecasts that total retail sales at current prices will increase by 22.8% between the end of 1997 and the year 2001. The largest increase will be in household goods (29%) as the housing market continues to improve. The lowest rate of increase is forecast for non-store retailing and repair (14.8%). Food will remain the largest sector, with its share of total retail sales forecast to decline marginally from 45.1% in 1997 to 44.9% in 2001. The share of total retail sales taken by household goods is forecast to increase from 12.7% in 1997 to 13.4% in 2001.

FT Retail & Consumer Publishing has been responsible for producing some of the more specialist reports on the future of retailing. One such example describes EDI (Electronic Data Interchange) and the reason for its introduction in the world of retailing.[12] There is a section on developments in UK retailing which looks at the changing role of retail businesses, the retail/supplier relationship, control of the distribution chain, international expansion and electronic shopping. Hendry analyses existing IT systems in retailing including point of sale systems, bar-coding and scanning and EFTPoS standards. As Hendry states, retailing has become polarised. Alongside a small number of very powerful chains, well financed and with international ambitions, there are many smaller shops operating within a local area or niche market. It is the existence of the large and powerful companies which has shaped, and to a large extent enabled, the emergence of EDI in retailing.

In another FT report, Gary Herman claims that there is considerable doubt as to the usefulness or profitability of so-called 'virtual stores' and 'cyber malls', and a large part of the reason for their success is undoubtedly the fact that electronic retailing formats are comparatively cheap rather than effective.[13] But that is significant in itself. Since it is possible with new technologies such as the World

Wide Web for a small retailer to reach a global market at very little cost, and since no-one really knows what will happen to consumer demand in the next few years, electronic retailing is already changing the nature of competition within retail. No single retailer on the Internet has market power.

The new electronic media – including home shopping TV channels, multimedia catalogues, online services and the Web – also help to illustrate a critical fact about contemporary retailing: it is increasingly a business concerned with marginal sales and niche markets. To dismiss electronic retailing because it represents only a small number of purchases and the media concerned have been oversold is to miss the point. Having cut margins to the bone as a result of deep recession and aggressive competition, retailers need to find new markets and new approaches. The new electronic retailing has two attractions, a favourable cost structure and access to non-traditional consumers.

The technologies to take non-store retailing further are all available, if neither as widespread nor as usable as the IT, communications and entertainment industries often claim. There is, according to Herman, still considerable doubt as to which carriers – digital TV, fibreoptic cable TV, telecommunications networks using a mix of copper and fibre, online networks, or something resembling the current Internet – will prevail in the electronic high street, and about what kind of technology will most appeal to users as a medium for electronic shopping.

The biggest problems for electronic retailing, whatever precise form it takes, are likely to be order processing and delivery. These will require a combination of new technologies, such as call centres and high-speed two-way communications links, and partnerships, to produce new methods for fulfilment. New media will also affect the way in which stores operate. From becoming pick-up points for customers purchasing groceries over the Internet to installing multimedia kiosks as store guides or automated shop assistants, the nature of stores will change. The new technologies will make stores more efficient in terms of their stockholding, floor area, staff-customer ratios and replenishment and reassortment processes. In fact, new technologies are creating infrastructure and applications which will eventually see the development of the 'intelligent store', but retailers are relatively slow to see the advantages of integrating different technologies such as EPoS, barcoding, intelligent shelf-edge labelling, kiosks, self-scanners and wireless networking to create a store in which functions can be automated or handed over to the shopper for greater efficiency, lower staffing, more accurate pricing and improved control of the supply chain. The reasons behind this reluctance are the costs involved, the relative experience of new technologies such as radio tags, and the legitimate doubts which experience indicates should be attached to the claims of technology vendors.

Herman feels the introduction of electronic cash and smart-card technologies will allow retailers to automate existing procedures and save money by reducing the costs of cash handling. On another level, electronic cash represents entirely new ways of doing business. There are broadly two aspects to electronic cash: the first is a method by which goods may be paid for electronically; the second is an improved method of paying for goods in stores. These two come together in the form of the electronic purse, a device based on smart-card technology, which can be charged with currency and used to pay for goods or services in stores or over communications links. The problem with electronic cash is that it will only be widely adopted if it combines the anonymity and convertibility of cash with the convenience and relative security of a credit card.

Information and communications technologies are playing an increasingly important role in retailing. Developments in this area have been pioneered by the Efficient Consumer Response (ECR) movement, which started in the US in the early 1990s and has now spread to the UK and mainland Europe. ECR started in grocery retailing as a movement to exploit the control of the supply chain that stores had developed, thanks to EDI and supplier partnerships, by feeding customer data into the process. In practice, ECR sought to integrate customer-focused IT systems with supplier-focused ones. A range of new technologies are available to help achieve this integration, starting with technologies for acquiring customer data in the first place (loyalty schemes, smart cards, new EPoS technologies), covering technologies for transmitting this data (new high-speed networks), but stopping at full-blown data warehouses using powerful new 'massively parallel processors' and sophisticated 'online analytical processing' tools to analyse information rapidly and detect trends which can be used to steer replenishment and reassortment to achieve something close to the ideal of 'just-in-time' delivery, based on supplier partnerships and the sort of flexible warehousing known as cross-docking.

Increasingly, the retailer is at the hub of a network of relationships with customers, staff and suppliers, and the retail outlet itself is taking on an entirely new character as a vehicle for distribution, not just a storehouse. Herman concludes that the biggest problems for retailers seeking to innovate and integrate will involve the implementation of technologies, not the technologies themselves. With IT becoming increasingly strategic to their business at every level, retailers might consider other partnerships, this time with IT suppliers. The report also contains interesting profiles of the corporate IT strategies employed by organisations such as Kwik Fit, Blackwells, Sears Roebuck and Giro Bank.

The market research publisher Mintel has described ECR as "the sharing of responsibilities and initiatives between different partners within the retail supply chain."[14] ECR comprises a number of proven grocery industry supply chain practices. These include category management, co-managed inventory, activity based costing, and computer assisted ordering, as well as cross-docking and others. In this *Special Report* Mintel looks at the way ECR takes all these individual elements and imposes a business process re-engineering framework over them. The aim is for a retail supply chain model which accommodates the changing patterns of consumer demand.

FT Retail have also published a report analysing the impact of ECR on the industry. Since the ECR Europe Executive Board first launched Efficient Consumer Response in Europe in 1996, there has been endless speculation about its significance for the grocery industry. Amidst the numerous interpretations, misconceptions and criticisms that surround ECR, Alan Mitchell attempts to assess its real value.[15] He offers an insight into ECR implementation across Europe, explaining why some companies see it as a breakthrough strategy and others are missing the point.

Mitchell is the foremost ECR commentator and, together with Coopers & Lybrand, he goes behind the scenes at those companies pioneering ECR to report on their experiences. Following two years of conducting pilot projects, the leading European ECR practitioners and consultants explain exactly how the principles of ECR are applied in Europe. The headline news in 1996 was that ECR would squeeze $33 billion of cost out of the European grocery supply chain. Now, the signs are that the first companies to come to terms with the demand side implications of ECR stand to generate similar percentage increases of incremental revenue. ECR is beginning to revolutionise trading relationships, marketing strategies and logistics across the industry.

The Institute of Grocery Distribution has produced a report which looks specifically at new technologies, key applications, business benefits, consumer benefits, survey results, supply chain implications and future developments in the grocery industry.[16] Electronic point-of-sale (EPoS) systems are among the most widely adopted in-store IT systems. IGD note that "usage of EPoS in grocery retailing is extensive and still expanding." EPoS systems help automate customer-billing at the checkout by scanning barcode labels on purchased items. Among the main benefits to the retailer are the elimination of the need to price products individually, improved checkout speeds and the possibility of using sales data in a central database to better understand consumers. For consumers, EPoS shortens checkout queues and provides itemised bills. Electronic customer counting and tracking (ECCaT) is often considered a useful add-on to EPoS. These systems use passive infra-red detectors or other devices to count the number of shoppers entering a store and then compare this with EPoS data. IGD note the development of other systems such as electronic shelf-labelling, although there has been a lack of enthusiasm for these systems in the UK. This is due primarily to the relatively high investment costs, the poor aesthetics of electronic labels and the risk of computer failure.

Prior to his work on *IT and the Future of Retail*, Herman had looked at the effects of information technology on the customer.[17] Here he considers that for the foreseeable future (five to ten years) retail operations will be subject to two overarching forces – the globalisation of the market and the need for customer-focus. In both of these areas information technology exerts a crucial influence. The success of retailers in the global market will depend on their ability to 'think globally and act locally.' The peculiar character of globalisation and customer-focus in retailing is technologically determined. Information technology has produced transaction processing and data communication infrastructures, and analytical and marketing tools, which will not just facilitate but define the forms of globalisation and customer-focus.

New technologies, both hardware and software, will help control the retail organisation, communicate with customers, facilitate promotional activity, and administer routine operations. According to Herman the most important of these technologies are:

- electronic point of sale (EPoS)
- electronic funds transfer (EFT or EFTPoS)
- smart cards
- bar-coding
- interactive multimedia
- CD-ROM
- virtual reality
- massively parallel processors
- data-mining

- rule induction
- neural nets
- electronic data interchange (EDI)
- satellite and wireless communications;
- new network infrastructures (e.g. structured cabling)
- electronic shelf-edge labelling
- computer telephony integration.

Many of these technologies have become commonplace in retail organisations since 1994 and taken together they have already transformed retailing. IT has allowed direct product pricing (DPP) and category management to change the face of many stores. EPoS networks, the single most important technological development in retailing, have enabled targeted marketing and sales promotion through the continuous analysis of sales transactions as they happen. The ultimate goal is 'micro-managing' – the control of store operations at shelf and sales counter level, even to focus on identifiable individual customers.

The convergence of IT and telecommunications promises the arrival of the virtual store, combining multimedia computing, high-speed data communications and computer-telephony integration. The success of home shopping TV channels and programmes, the growth of telephone-based retailing, the spread of warehouse clubs, and the increasingly evident cross-border activities of many retailers are pointers to a future which may not be as imminent as IT enthusiasts often make out, but which cannot be indefinitely delayed. However, size or reach alone do not guarantee success and retailing's recent past has demonstrated that growth may bring as many problems as it solves. Increasingly, retailers must learn to maximise the choice they offer customers, enter partnerships with suppliers (and even with competitors), be prepared to diversify, and adjust their market positioning frequently and rapidly. Writing at the same time as Herman, Tony Savage looks at EPoS 2000 and considers what is likely to be offered to the retailer by the year 2000.[18] He evaluates both the in-store EPoS system and suppliers in the year 2000, as well as providing profiles of the major suppliers.

The market research publisher Euromonitor has also offered its' view on the shape of retailing in the year 2000.[19] The main volume of *European Retail Structures* provides an excellent strategic management overview of the retail trade. The recommendations to the retail trade are supported by an analysis of the operating environment and the legislative framework. The sections on recent and forthcoming legislation, shopping hours and retail development, lead into a general European overview including trends in retail sales. Key retailing issues such as changing shopping habits, the growth in out-of-town sites and locations, environmental influences, distance shopping and franchising are all considered. Euromonitor also look at the key technological issues from electronic point-of-purchase systems through to digital shelf-pricing systems. The section on new trading concepts highlights discounters, warehouse clubs, factory outlets, category killers, catalogue showrooms, and specialist and theme catalogues. Following a discussion of corporate retail strategies, such as diversification and cost reduction, Euromonitor conclude with their prospects for the retail trade to the year 2000.

Mintel have produced a range of *Special Reports* looking at recent developments in the retail trade. One of these analyses the entrance of supermarkets into the financial services field.[20] As well as considering the diversification of supermarkets into previously unchartered territory, there is a look at the 'one-stop' shop and the structure of retailing in the UK. There are surveys of consumer preferences for 'one-stop' shopping as Mintel try to predict the likely success of supermarkets selling financial products.

One of the big trends in retailing in recent years has been the increasing emphasis on customer loyalty. Mintel provide marketing profiles of the major players and look at patterns of shopping and secondary shopping.[21] There is consideration of the basis of loyalty and the ways in which retailers might exploit customer disloyalty. Following an analysis of retailer initiatives and views on what the shopper really wants, Mintel predicts the future use of loyalty schemes. Mintel build upon this report in a later publication which profiles the winners and losers in the grocery retail sector.[22] Here Mintel stress the importance of diversification and proliferation of the product range, development of the own label and new product development, and a change in pricing tactics. In order to maintain market position grocery retailers need to employ increasing diversity in promotional tactics and campaigns. The speed of development in the sector is reflected in constantly changing store formats.

In 1996 Mintel produced two *Special Reports* on the topical subject of customer loyalty. The first confronts the question, what are the driving forces for improvement in retailing?[23] There is a detailed consideration of customer service and the need for higher service standards in shops. Can retailers maintain market position without paying full attention to the demands of the customer? The question of loyalty, according to Mintel, begins with getting the basics right. The second provides a general overview of customer loyalty in retailing.[24] Mintel analyse the degree of participation in leading loyalty schemes and look at some of the more popular schemes in operation. There is an insight into strategy, tactics and shopper behaviour which takes in the various aspects of customer loyalty: loyalty through empathy; loyalty to locality; price driven loyalty; pragmatic loyalty and so on.

The big three retailers, Safeway, Sainsbury's and Tesco, have all implemented data warehousing technology to enable them to collate and analyse details of shopping purchases throughout the country. Information is gathered via the loyalty cards – an increasingly common device in the retail sector. These cards identify the shopper and enable their purchases to be recorded every time they visit. Customers are rewarded for using their cards through points giving discounts and other incentives. The amount of information involved is staggering. Safeway installed a data warehouse for its loyalty card scheme, *ABC*, in mid-1995. During that time, the company has built a collection of around 7.5 billion records from its 6 million card holders. Safeway expects this to grow to between 10 and 12 billion records after two years. Tesco's *Clubcard* system, launched in February 1995, has more than five million active members and is building a similar data store for the retailer.

Information collected at Safeway checkouts is stored in computers in each of the company's 400 stores. Once stored, sophisticated tools are used to analyse the data and extract information on buying habits and trends. Listing all the customers who have bought a product on more than one occasion over the previous year takes about an hour – a process involving a search of five to six billion records. It is this capability to analyse vast quantities of data which has led to major retailers embracing the technology so enthusiastically. The individual transactions alone are of little interest, but given enough of them, the trends they show can be invaluable. Product associations are one area which has particularly excited retailers. Finding links between seemingly unrelated items – beer and nappies, for example – might allow a store to increase sales by moving items closer together or offering discounts when purchased as a pair. This type of correlation would not have been possible without a data warehouse.

A better relationship equals better sales and retailers are constantly looking to their data warehouses to suggest new ways this can be achieved. Sales data is often compared with information from other sources, such as market research companies, to better understand what makes shoppers tick. Customers are categorised into life stages – single people, married couples, families and retired people – and their theoretical buying habits compared with those seen in store. This is marketing at a micro level.

In a comprehensive report for FT Retail, Sue Rayner examines and analyses customer loyalty schemes – what they are, and how they fit into the wider context of the marketing mix.[25] The report helps to identify which scheme is right for particular organisations, offers advice on how to measure scheme success and pinpoints problems of fraud and security. With analysis of the implications of new technologies and data warehousing, the report contains the information required to develop closer and more responsive relationships with customers. Finally, Rayner offers useful case studies of the schemes employed by Tesco, Argos and Shell.

A useful annual review of retailing appears in the journal *Retail Trade Review*, formerly published by the Economist Intelligence Unit but now under the auspices of Corporate Intelligence on Retailing. The review summarises the year in retailing and looks at future prospects for the retail trade. For example, the 1996 review shows that the growth in the underlying level of retail sales fell sharply in 1995, with sales volume ahead by only 1.2%, one-third of the 3.7% gain of 1994.[26] This brought to an end three successive years of improving volume growth rates from the low point of 1991 and signalled a clear loss of momentum in the retail recovery. For the fifth successive year, large retail businesses recorded markedly stronger results than small businesses in 1995. The former added 6% to turnover as volume increased by 3%, while the latter suffered a 2% drop in turnover as volume contracted by 4%. It became clear very early in 1995 that the retail recovery was losing momentum and, although trading picked up after a very poor first couple of months, the year as a whole proved disappointing. Corporate Intelligence analyse the reasons for the poor set of figures and explain why the prospects for an up-turn in 1996 were that much brighter.

Mintel have looked in detail at lifestage group characterstics and shopper priorities and behaviour.[27] As well as reporting sector by sector from food and clothes shopping through to DIY and gardening products, Mintel consider the expectations of shops and shopping and highlight lifestage and segmentation strategies. A similar report from Taylor Nelson AGB explores the gains and losses in consumer spend for each grocery retailer.[28] The report also includes detailed analysis of consumer behaviour based on Superpanel survey results.

Convenience retailing is one of the fastest growing concepts in the UK grocery industry. New convenience stores are being developed and existing grocery stores are being converted to a convenience format throughout the country. Though not a new phenomenon (Sperrings were trading from what is generally recognised as the UK's first convenience store in the early seventies and 7-Eleven opened their first

British store in Hendon in 1984), the adoption of a convenience format has been seen by many as the only way that smaller grocery stores can survive, and even thrive, in the mid to late 90's.

The billions of pounds poured into developing superstores on the edges of all towns and cities has created enormous competititve pressures for grocery retailers trading out of smaller stores. It has proved impossible for them to compete against the scale and expertise of Tesco, Sainsbury's, Safeway and Asda. The smaller grocer does not have the buying power and cannot achieve the economies of scale that are available to the major multiples. Hence their prices appear uncompetitive and trade is lost with little likelihood of it ever being recouped. Coupled with this has been an increasing number of discounters trading in the UK. Kwik-Save have continued to grow store numbers, whilst the entry of Netto, Aldi and Lidl to the UK market has increased the pressures on smaller grocers. The role of the traditional grocer on a high street or shopping parade has become marginalised. To survive in such a harsh competitive environment, differentiation has been the key driver behind the rise of convenience.

Convenience stores offer longer trading hours, large impulse ranges, basic groceries, a focal point for communities and easier/friendlier places for consumers to shop. The evolution of convenience concepts is at an early stage. Numbers of stores and the ranges carried within them are continually developing. Operators in this sector are involved in an on-going race both to stay ahead of their sector competitors but also to keep abreast of the multiples who are continually improving trading offers. The race has already seen some casualties but clearly too there have been winners. Barnes and Dadomo have evaluated how the race is progressing and in what direction it is likely to proceed.[29] Their report looks at how the so-called 'top-up shop' is battling in its attempt to survive the growth of the out-of-town superstore. The convenience store hopes to develop a niche that exists within the UK grocery market for the top-up shop conducted by consumers in between superstore visits.

Mike Phillips has also produced a strategic review of the UK convenience store market.[30] He discusses the evolution of convenience retailing in the UK from its humble beginnings in Lancashire in 1844, with the Rochdale Pioneers, through to today when there are in excess of 262,000 C-stores. Phillips considers C-store strategies currently in operation worldwide and examines the changing dynamics of the industry, focusing especially on the way consumer lifestyles are evolving. The strength of Phillips' report lies in the case studies of the leading C-stores such as Spar, Tesco Metro, Shell Select, T&S Stores, M+W and Londis. These UK companies are compared with 7-Eleven in Japan, arguably the world's leading C-store operator, in order to provide a benchmark of performance criteria.

With the big five supermarket chains accounting for virtually all weekly shopping the C-store is being forced to redefine what it has on offer. Many independents have given up – some 185,000 shops have disappeared in the period 1950-1995 – as the many boarded-up local shop parades highlight. The London Chamber of Commerce has suggested the situation will get even worse and a recent survey by the Asian Business Forum indicated that more than 70% of independent store owners did not expect to be in business 10 years from now. In order to survive into the next century Phillips believes the C-store will have to adopt measures that:

- recognise that convenience itself is not enough
- provide excellent personal service and commitment to the community or client base
- understand that businesses need to be managed effectively, with the adoption of such supply techniques as efficient consumer response
- provide management with information about their businesses and markets by using the latest information technology
- give thought to the future product assortment and involve close liaison with manufacturers.

They will also need to become:

- aligned to a larger voluntary buying group e.g. Spar, Mace
- part of a franchise e.g. 7-Eleven
- part of an integrated supply chain e.g. Alldays, Dillons.

In addressing the industry's pressing issues, Phillips provides vital information on retail strategies employed globally, emerging formats, and new opportunities for achieving sustainable competitive advantage. Loyalty schemes and own label product ranges are among the strategies deployed by convenience store groups to position themselves as niche retailers rather than distress purchase destinations. The incisive case studies examine the strategies that will dominate the future direction of the convenience store sector.

The desire to become 'all things to all people' has culminated in the leading superstores trying to break into the market for financial services. Datamonitor, the market research analyst, has produced a report containing case studies on each superstore, describing the innovative retailing methods employed.[31] For example, the study on Tesco analyses its *Clubcard* scheme, out-of-town shopping, the replenishment and distribution system, petrol stations, share dealing services and shopping direct.

The ultimate 'one-stop' concept has seen the major superstores establish personal savings accounts, loans, mortgages and a range of other financial services. The new Sainsbury's Bank has been exceeding all targets. It now has 500,000 customers and £1 billion on deposit. Cash is flowing in at £50 per second and 12,000 new accounts are opened per week. Nearly three quarters of the bank's new customers are recruited from Sainsbury's Reward card loyalty scheme, and there are 10 million cards in circulation, which are used for 80% of sales.

In 1997 Tesco Personal Finance installed its own-brand cash machines in 120 Tesco stores and eventually hopes to have machines in all stores. This is the first step towards the introduction of a Tesco Bank, which will offer full banking facilities through modern style branches – "without the cathedral atmosphere you experience in traditional banks", according to a spokesman. Sainsbury's Bank opened its own-brand cash machines at six supermarkets in September 1997, with plans to open them across its chain of 381 supermarkets. Sainsbury's Bank is ahead of Tesco Personal Finance in terms of the number of services it offers, but has yet to offer full banking facilities, although these are promised "within the next two years." Sainsbury's operates its range of financial services primarily over the phone and has no plans to introduce branches, instead prefering to ape the successful First Direct approach to banking. At present most its' customers appear to be attracted by good savings rates but if the supermarkets launch current accounts at the right price then the banks are likely to see widescale defections.

A survey carried out for Shell UK showed almost 17 million people shop in the evening and 5 million shop after 10pm.[32] Most night shoppers are men buying items such as cigarettes, milk or soft drinks. Most people still continue to do the weekly shop during the day, but late-night impulse shopping is increasing. The survey revealed 17 million, or 37% of adults, shop after 8pm at least once a week; 5 million shop after 10pm at least once a week. Some 56% of the adults surveyed said that they felt positive towards a 24-hour society. Most of those questioned would like to see shops, restaurants and supermarkets stay open later. 71% said they shopped late at least once a week, the most common reason given was having either forgotten something, run short of an item, or just finished work. 22% of those questioned said they shopped between 10pm and 3am because they were working full time and this was the only time they had available. Just over half of those taking part said they went late night shopping at petrol station forecourt shops; 31% used corner shops, and 7% went to supermarkets. Only 5% said that they had come to a Shell 24 garage at a late hour to buy petrol.

Aside from the advent of online shopping, what's in store for the traditional avenues of retailing?

- The view from Verdict is that the best performing sectors over the five years 1997 to 2001 will be those associated with consumer electronics (computers especially) as a new generation of electronic leisure products looms. Market leaders Dixons and Comet are well placed to reap the benefits.
- A modest quickening in the housing market (still only two thirds of 1988 levels in Verdict's forecast) will provide some uplift for furnishings, housewares, DIY, and household appliances.
- Department stores are again tipped for better times, under the twin influences of demographics (making for an ageing population) and the wave of new openings planned by the big names over the next five years.
- Superstores will continue to dominate the grocery trade, as store extensions and the cultivation of wider non-food ranges make up for a combination of lighter planning restrictions and shrinkage in the reservoir of good sites as the out-of-town development wave moves well beyond its peak. Sport retailers may be the next group of non-food specialists to come under pressure from the big grocers "if superstores can gain access to reliable supplies," says Verdict.[33]

The tenth edition of the annual reference work *Retail Rankings* covers 700 companies and 1,250 retail operations in context.[34] The work identifies and ranks the leading 700 retailers in the UK by turnover and various other indicators of size and performance. More detailed comparative information on retail groups and operations is provided in the 37 sub-sector rankings. Included here, as usual, are sub-sector and market share estimates for the leading companies and other market-oriented data. Also presented is comparative information on companies' stockturn and the proportion of their sales spent on staff remuneration. *Retail Rankings* remains an essential publication for the level of retail market analysis and indication of shifts in power amongst the leading retailers. In addition to listing the top 100 retailers in the UK and the leading UK retailers by sector, there are tables of leading multi-sector retailers and British-owned retailers. The section on acquisitions and mergers offers the opportunity to track activity in the sector during the period 1989-1996 and provides a table of the top 50 acquisitions.

Table 3.1 Top 10 Retailers

1.	J. Sainsbury Plc
2.	Tesco Plc
3.	Safeway Plc
4.	Marks & Spencer Plc
5.	Asda Group Plc
6.	Kingfisher Plc
7.	Boots Company Plc
8.	Somerfield Plc
9.	Kwik Save Group Plc
10.	John Lewis Partnership Plc

Between 1986 and 1996 retail sales grew by 74%, from £87.2 billion to £151.6 billion but, rather more interestingly, those of the top 10 ranked multiples advanced by 155%, from £22.7 billion to £57.5 billion. This increasing concentration – the top 10's share of all sales rose from 26 to 36% and the top 100's from 55 to 69% – has been a marked feature of the period and of successive editions of *Retail Rankings*.

Despite the disappearance of a few household names along the way, such as Fine Fare and Bejam, and significant restructuring by means of acquisition, the old guard has held its own tolerably well since 1985/86. Sainsbury's, Marks & Spencer, Tesco, Asda (then with MFI), Somerfield (then known as Dee), a pre-Kingfisher Woolworth, Boots and Argyll (Safeway) were then, as now, stalwarts of the top 10 (GUS and ABF were the other two ten years ago). Another aspect of the last ten years has been the massive investment in new stores – many of them out-of-town – and in new technology. The report includes figures offering performance comparisons for selected major UK retailers between 1985/86 and 1995/96.

Another essential reference tool for retailers is the *Retail Directory*. Established in 1939, and now into its 52nd edition, the directory remains a key source for contact details within the retail trade.[35] The directory contains chapters on trade associations and professional bodies; department stores and principal shops; multiple shops; large retail groups; department store groups; co-operative societies; out-of-town shopping; cash and carry; voluntary associations; mail order firms; concessions; shopping centres and precincts; new shopping centre developments; factory outlet centres; airport/railway shopping; town centre management; retail journals. There are also countrywide shopping street surveys. The *out-of-town shopping* section covers those companies who trade from large units on the periphery of towns and cities. Generally these sites take the form of retail parks with parking and additional facilities. Over the last few years an increasing number of firms have turned to retailing in these 'edge-of-town' or 'retail park' locations, some as an alternative and some in addition to high street activities. The directory uses the term 'out-of-town' shopping to cover all these types of retailing and includes companies operating hypermarkets and superstores, as these are considered precursors of a general trade.

"Today's supermarket is the old high street under one roof." So says Richard Hyman of retail analysts Verdict Research. His company's report on *Grocers & Supermarkets* looks at the market in terms of grocery store numbers, grocers share of the food retail market and overall grocers sales.[36] The report also contains profiles on the leading grocers. The grocery sector is the largest component of the UK retail industry. Some 38p in every pound spent in British shops passes through a grocery store. This dominance has not come simply because people have to eat – total grocers' sales of £64 billion is 25% larger than the food market. The position that grocers occupy today has come through successfully anticipating consumer trends and evolving their store formats to increase their appeal to shoppers.

The repeal of Resale Price Maintenance in 1964 enabled retailers to adopt discounting strategies. Self-service stores were much less labour intensive than service ones and facilitated cost cutting. This set up virtuous circles where greater efficiency led to lower prices which improved sales volumes, which in turn enhanced efficiency and grew buying power. This process encouraged the growth of successful multiples.

The original self-service store developed into supermarkets throughout the 1960s and 1970s. Average store size needed to track upwards in order to accommodate an explosion of product choice as the mass consumer economy developed. These trends led to the development of large superstores which have increasingly replaced supermarkets over the past twenty years or so.

The main phase of superstore development is now over as saturation approaches and attention is turning to refurbishing existing outlets and enhancing the facilities and services on offer. Grocers are also exploiting opportunities on the high street (eg Tesco Metro) or petrol forecourt C-stores (Tesco Express, Safeway/BP). Capturing more of the spending of existing loyal customers is the development strategy being pursued, leading to the introduction of pharmacies, post offices, petrol, and so on, to further exploitation of non-food markets and possibly to doctor's surgeries, sale of gas/electricity and financial services products. The number of superstores will not change much going forward nor will store size, but service based competition will not be any less intense.

The growth of supermarkets and then superstores over the past thirty years has led to grocery spending consolidating into fewer, but larger outlets. This has led to a dramatic reduction in the number of grocery outlets although the majority of this attrition occurred in the 1960s, 1970s and 1980s.

Grocery Store Numbers 1961-1996

Year	Number 000	Index
1961	147	100
1971	105	71
1980	58	40
1990	43	29
1991	41	28
1992	40	27
1993	40	27
1994	33*	na
1995	32*	na
1996	31*	na

*Revised ONS classifications

Source: IGD, ONS, Verdict Analysis

In terms of absolute numbers, the independents have suffered most closures but there has also been substantial pruning amongst the multiples and Co-ops of older, smaller stores. Over recent years most of the majors have increased store numbers. The exception is Argyll (now Safeway) which has been cutting its tail of small Presto and Safeway stores and has sold off the Lo-Cost discount operation.

The standard definition for 'superstores' is of food based stores with a sales area greater than 25,000 sq. ft. on one floor and with adjacent parking facilities. Development opportunites for superstores were boosted from the mid 1980s when the government relaxed planning constraints. The grocery retailers saw this as a window of opportunity that might be closed and so there has been a surge of development activity over the past ten years. Although the government now claims to have tightened up out-of-town planning, superstore development is still proceeding at a vigorous pace and it is a shortage of really good superstore sites that will be the main constraint on future expansion. The day of food superstore saturation is not that far distant.

Super Store Numbers 1986-1996

Year	Numbers at year end
1986	457
1987	500
1988	578
1989	644
1990	733
1991	803
1992	860
1993	934
1994	988
1995	1027
1996	1060

Source: Verdict Analysis

The above table indicates the acceleration of openings in the mid-1980s (78 in 1988; 89 in 1990; 74 in 1993) and the subsequent slowdown (39 in 1995; 33 in 1996). The pace of superstore openings going forward will continue to track downwards as suitable site opportunities dry up. Further closures of Co-op superstores and replacements of old Asdas will constrain overall numbers. Growth will come from refurbishments and extensions to existing stores to give smaller superstores the ability to stock a full product range.

Dr Ross Davies has edited a comprehensive review of retailing in western Europe: especially its economies, trends and issues in terms of efficiency, quality and profitability.[37] This FT Retail report identifies common themes and key issues across the continent, and examines retailers' responses to them. Leading European experts discuss the increasing domination by large format multiple retailers; growing uniformity in high streets across Europe; convergence in entertainment and retail activities and the trend to specialisation. The report addresses issues surrounding the retail industry such as: changing retail structures; changing retailer/supplier relationships; information technology developments; the in-town/out-of-town development debate; the so-called green issues; demographic and socio-economic issues; changing power relationships in the process of distribution; and, finally, future prospects.

'Category killers' have only recently arrived in the UK.[38] A category killer is essentially a retailer who specialises in one clearly defined product category and aims to offer the maximum possible range of stock in that category. This relatively new phenomenon arose in response to the ever-increasing cost of high quality retail space, as a way of achieving the necessary volume to cover costs without losing the benefits to the customer of specialising in a particular product area. The prime benefit to the customer of specialising in a particular product category is the ability to maintain a comprehensive range of stock, and it is this feature of their format that is given most prominence by category killers. The large-format sites required by category killers usually mean that they are found in relatively cheap locations away from town centres. Some category killers, such as Olympus Sportsworld, are in fact offshoots of town centre retailers. Running a dual facia chain such as this enables a conventional retailer to compete with category killers, or just to take advantage of the drift towards out-of-town retailing without having to abandon its established retail strategy.

The out-of-town orientation of category killers imposes certain requirements on the detail of their locations. To guarantee constant customer traffic category killers generally aim to be located close to large-format grocers or other retailers, such as Marks and Spencer, which attract constant shopping. This is beginning to lead to the type of out-of-town retail development seen in the US, where out-of-town sites become clusters of specialist retailers, known as 'power centres'. This trend may well hasten the passing of legislation on a national as well as on a pan-European scale to counter the drift of retailing away from town centres. Smith's report analyses the position of the category killer retail format in Europe. It examines the reasons why this format has developed, its origins in the US, and its prospects for further development in Europe.

NTC produce a useful pocket-sized compendium of retail facts and figures. Published in association with AC Nielsen, the *Retail Pocket Book* also contains a section on 'Developments in Retailing'.[39] As well as listing the top retailers worldwide there are details on retail concentration, retail scanning and trends in home shopping. There are also sections on retail crime and prevention, retail advertising and international retailing.

Since 1978 Hillier Parker has published a comprehensive listing of shopping centre developments in Britain of more than 50,000 sq. ft. gross.[40] All 759 town centre and 'out-of-town' located shopping centres opened over the 1965-1994 period are included in the 1995 edition. To aid in the updating of shopping centre records, questionnaires are distributed to all centre owners on an annual basis. These regular surveys have allowed the collection of a range of supplementary information useful for benchmarking purposes: for example, vacancy rates, visitor numbers, anchor distributions, parking and food court provisions. Hillier Parker confirm that shopping centre development activity remains at a very low ebb. Given the apparent cross-party support for the Government's anti-out-of-town shopping stance, it seems very unlikely that any further major out-of-town regional centres will obtain planning consent.

The report contains some fascinating results:

- 70 shopping centres are located out-of-town.
- there are 25 shopping centres in Britain of more than 500,000 sq. ft.
- just 7 shopping centres opened during 1994, the lowest number of openings recorded since the series began in 1965.
- Boots the Chemist is represented in more shopping centres than any other store trader.

One of the greatest changes to retailing in the UK during recent years has been the advent of Sunday opening. Healey & Baker have been monitoring the effect of Sunday trading on a cross-section of multiple retailers since its legislation on the 28 August 1994. They have produced a brief report summarising which shops are opening and who is shopping on Sundays.[41] There is a look at particular retailers' experiences and a consideration of the property implications. They conclude that Sunday trading has settled down into a more established seasonal pattern with peaks occurring pre-Christmas and again in the summer, although only time will tell. It would appear that Sunday trading is largely re-arranging the same real level of spending, rather than generating additional consumer expenditure.

Those retailers who have benefited from Sunday trading acknowledge that the increase in profitability has only been marginal and variable over time. A number of retailers admit that their profits have not increased much, if at all. The most obvious winners are free-standing supermarkets and out-of-town retail warehouses, together with the regional shopping centres. Sales are being poached from those retailers not opening and from town centres where there is insufficient critical mass. The planned shopping centres are therefore clear winners.

Healey & Baker have recently updated their survey to show that three years following its introduction, Sunday shopping has overtaken other more traditional pastimes on the day of rest. More than one in two Britons now go shopping on a Sunday – while only 12% of Britons regularly sit down to a traditional Sunday meal with the family. The opportunity to shop on Sunday is greater than ever, with towns and cities continuing to push Sunday trading. Since 1996 the number of stores open for trading on Sunday has increased by 6%. Newcastle, Leicester and Stoke have all launched Sunday opening, while Bath, Bristol, Cambridge and Manchester all saw a considerable increase in the number of open shops.

According to the most recent Healey & Baker survey, twenty-two of the top 25 towns and cities are now open every Sunday and 65% of the top 100. It is principally the large regional shopping centres, such as Lakeside, Meadowhall and Metro Centre, and major cities such as Manchester, Birmingham and London's West End which are open. Again it appears that Sunday trading is largely rearranging the same level of weekly consumer expenditure, rather than generating additional expenditure. Forty-five percent of retailers trading on Sunday reported that they had seen no additional profits from Sunday trading. The average increase in profits was only just over 1%. But though it may not lead to increased profits for retailers, those that are not open run the risk of losing out.

There are lessons here, says Healey & Baker, for retailers considering extended hours shopping throughout the whole week. So far, very few retailers are open regularly after 8.00pm and virtually none (except some of the supermarkets and convenience stores) have toyed with 24 hour shopping. Most say that the level of expenditure does not justify the cost of opening – the same argument that many retailers used on the introduction of Sunday trading, but until a large number of stores are open late, it is difficult to judge the potential demand. The probabilty is that the marginal return on costs is unlikely to be worthwhile after 9.00pm.

The survey shows that supermarkets fare the best of all on Sundays – 81% of Sunday shoppers in England and Wales buy food and groceries – while the traditional out-of-town Sunday favourites – DIY centres and garden centres – come in second (21%) and third (20%) respectively. Sunday trading accounts for an average turnover of around 37% of Saturday sales, according to retailers. Sales are being poached from those retailers that are not opening and from town centres that do not have enough open shops to attract a critical mass of shoppers.

Fifty-five percent of English and Welsh respondents to the survey shop on Sunday – the same as in 1996. A larger proportion of Scots shop on a Sunday (62%). Most shop at least two or three times a month. The frequency of Sunday shopping is greatest in Scotland, the South East, South West and East Anglia, and lowest in Wales and Yorkshire & Humberside. But 45% of Britons still do not go shopping on a Sunday. Of those, the majority (55%) say they just prefer to do other things, while 9% do not go shopping on a Sunday because they are morally opposed to it.

More than half of Sunday shoppers spend less than £20 and around a third spend less than £10; little change on 1996 results. The highest spenders are from the West Midlands, with an average of £36 (up 50% on 1996). Londoners spend on average £33, the Welsh £32, followed by the South West £31. Sunday shoppers from Yorkshire & Humberside spend the least (£20).

In the UK and Europe the potential of roadside retailing is growing and evolving along a number of interesting parallels. Although some years behind the US, the spiritual home of the gas station, forecourt retailing represents one of the fastest growth areas in retail across Europe. Such is the potential of oil company roadside real estate, that in many markets, profits from fuel sales are eclipsed by profits from the ever-growing numbers of products which constitute a viable forecourt sale, and as that number grows so the potential of these sites has increased in line.

Bracey-Gibbon and Graham have considered the long-term consequences of new partnerships flooding the forecourt sector.[42] Oil majors are investing heavily in forecourt development and entering into strategic alliances with retailers, thus securing necessary levels of expertise in both fields. Their report details the growth of the product mix and new marketing opportunities that these mergers present for both oil companies and retailers. The *Future of Forecourt Retailing: a Roadside Retail Boom* reveals the latest market distribution forecasts for the industry, analysing the future relationships between oil majors, retailers, supermarket petrol retailers and independent dealers.

An earlier report from Market Assessment (MAPS) had also looked at the retailing of petrol and convenience retailing, and analysed the marriage of the two areas into a major growth phenomenon.[43] Whilst concentrating on the UK market the report does consider developments in the USA and other parts of Europe and comments upon the key environmental issues faced by the oil suppliers.

Retailing is becoming an increasingly global business. Fewer numbers of ever larger companies are exercising significant influence on the retail market. Various factors are responsible for this trend, some prompting retailers to expand overseas and others attracting retailers to look further than their existing domestic horizons. Consumer, technology and market factors prompt retailers to consider cross-border retailing. Through the increasing ease and cost-effectiveness of international travel, consumers have been exposed to a huge variety of foreign products, and this has influenced the range of goods offered by many retailers. Also, the speed of information exchange through advanced technology has enabled retailers to establish, run and analyse cross-border businesses far more effectively than ever before.

Cross-border retailers pursue various principal methods of expansion including chain acquisitions and equity stakes; organic (greenfield and site acquisition); joint ventures; franchising, licensing, distributors and agents; mail order; concessions; alliances; and cross-currency retailing. White has assessed the companies that have applied these various techniques and examined how some have been successful and others not.[44] This includes both the strategy used to enter the specific market, and the management style and/or product mix. Many of the answers lie in the ability of companies to take risks. Analysis is carried out to compare companies in similar businesses with a view to finding the formula which has produced the best results regardless of the industry concerned.

White's report examines the cross-border retail industry from a global perspective, but focuses particularly on the US, European and Asian markets. It is divided into nine chapters: the first three look at the reasons, strategies, issues, and developments of the cross-border phenomenon; the following five are a review of some major cross-border sectors; and the final chapter provides a summary and conclusions.

The retail industry is about to be revolutionised by a tidal wave of new technology and business practices. Electronic transactions will replace the more familiar forms of cash and cheque in many instances. Soon it will be possible for credit/debit card sales to be completed in three seconds without the need for a signature. At the same time, the long awaited boom in electronic commerce, using the Internet, is going to give many outlets the opportunity to introduce value-added services that will enable customers to do things such as place orders while still at work and collect their purchases on the way home.

Start and Phillips have written a report for FT Retail that examines the new technologies and business practices behind these changes and explains what they are, who is supporting them, when they will be introduced and how they will affect retailers at all levels.[45] With this information, retailers will be able to determine and integrate their strategies for the future. There are two distinct areas where changes are going to take place: the incorporation of smartchip technology into the existing forms of credit/debit, cheque guarantee and automated teller machine (ATM) cards; and the evolution of electronic commerce. The boundaries between these two disparate forms of electronic transaction are currently well defined. However, within a relatively short period of time these boundaries will blur.

There is an in-depth analysis of every aspect of the payment card revolution from smartchips to the EMV (Europay/mastercard/Visa) standard to multi-function cards. Their report takes a close look at the so-called 'cashless society'. It is no longer a case of 'if' change will take place, but how soon it will happen. Certainly the timeframe has been established for the introduction of chipcard technology, with pilots all over the world before the end of 1997 and full roll-out was scheduled for 1998. Customer acceptance will follow rapidly as individuals become aware of the benefits of the new systems. The direct involvement of retailers will be a crucial element of this acceptance.

Start & Phillips investigate the claim that shops, as we know them now, will cease to exist within the next 20 years. One of the case studies they use to highlight the shift towards electronic commerce is the pilot 'Home Shopper' scheme introduced by Tesco. Off-line browsing at the products and on-line ordering keeps shopping with 'Home Shopper' cheap and quick, with the software accepting all major debit and credit cards. Tesco plans to implement efficient home delivery before expanding the trial – it will be interesting to see if other retailers can keep pace with the supermarket giant.

Home delivery could change the face of supermarket shopping as we know it, with enormous financial consequences for the companies and their investors. Most of the market leaders have been experimenting with some kind of delivery service. Sainsbury's has probably gone further than any, in association with an independent delivery company, Flanagan, in south London. But even this is a barely noticeable dipping of toes in the water. Now that Microsoft boss, Bill Gates, has forecast that a third of shopping will be carried out from home by the year 2005, a head of steam is building up behind the idea. Consultants Arthur Andersen say a fifth of all grocery shopping could be carried out in this way.

With an ageing population, and widespread dislike of trailing round supermarkets even by those who are fit and able to do so, there is clearly some logic in such predictions, even if you do not share Bill Gates' belief in the Internet. However, it is completely at odds with the rapid decline in doorstep sales of the one product which is still provided in this fashion – milk; and the logistics of home delivery are nightmarish. A week's groceries cannot be left on the doorstep like the morning milk, or dumped next door, as is the practice with some mail order companies. Deliverers are therefore left with the prospect of repeat journeys, adding to cost, which is in any case an impediment to the spread of such a service.

Other variants seem more viable, such as delivery to office buildings or drive-through collection, but one way or another it is now becoming accepted that supermarkets will lose a substantial proportion of their checkout sales. That is good news for shoppers tired of queuing, and for the companies, which have had to pour money into extra checkout service in pursuit of "one in front" promises to customers. But it has serious financial consequences. Modern supermarketing is based on the model of expensive superstores, which justify their cost because of the sales densities they achieve. Take out a third or a fifth of the shoppers and those sales densities start to plummet. Good news for the remaining customers who will then be able to travel the aisles in a more leisurely fashion, but bad news for the value of the stores.

There has already been one round of property write-downs in the sector, when it became obvious that the superstore bonanza was ending and accounting treatments had been too optimistic. But a rapid reduction in the number of people actively shopping in superstores would lead to a much more substantial hit. As well as this direct financial threat, home shopping poses a more fundamental danger for the superstore business. Once the direct link between shopper and store is broken, there is a good chance that shopping will become more fragmented, just as in the days before supermarkets when shops used to deliver.

Supermarkets have put smaller specialists out of business because it is just so convenient to buy meat and vegetables in the same place at the same time as the baked beans and cornflakes. But if the baked beans and cornflakes are being delivered by Sainsbury's, the convenience factor diminishes. Remote buying is bound to be less attractive for fresh food, and it is easy to imagine a pattern of shopping which combines a delivery of packaged groceries with visits to butchers and greengrocers – where they still exist. Home delivery could be a way for superstores to provide better service, but it could also be a route back to the days of more varied shopping, with the supermarket companies losing out on the most profitable segment of fresh food.

Evidence is building elsewhere of the growing significance of e-commerce, although its impact is patchy as yet. In *The Future of Shopping*, Julian Markham comments that, significantly, retailers are continuing to invest heavily in their traditional activities – more, bigger and better outlets, and he predicts that catalogue shopping from leading high street stores is likely to expand.[46] But he finds little mention of the Internet other than as a promotional medium. "Is this a head-in-the-sand response from a tired industry," he asks, "or a sound proposition based on a well-founded confidence in consumers' desire to shop personally?"

E-commerce is rightly associated with the ongoing development of the 'information society', where value is measured and corporate profitability determined by an enterprise's ability to capture, assimilate, manage and distribute information. This can be readily seen in the greatly increased importance being attached to customer care programmes. Capturing customers and maintaining their loyalty is essential for survival in an increasingly competitive world. It can also be seen in distribution and support functions which increasingly are carried out globally. E-commerce encompasses all this functionality – advertising, capturing customers, managing customers, distribution and support – as well as the actual financial transaction side of corporate business. In short, it involves a totality of business processes. Dedman's recent report provides a framework, a model, for understanding this totality of e-commerce.[47] The model is applied consistently throughout the report and draws on case studies, best industry practice, leading-edge e-commerce products, and actual corporate usage to illustrate and expand on the presented framework. In addition it provides market projections, analysis of leading suppliers, and a detailed look at how regulators in Europe are already seeking to manage the perceived threats and opportunities of e-commerce.

E-commerce has already arrived in a big way in the US. Globally, online advertising is the herald of e-commerce activity. Internet advertising revenue is expected to have reached the US$1 billion mark by the end of 1997 – an annual growth rate approaching 400%. Jupiter Communications, a New York communications research group, estimates that online advertisement spending should reach US$7.7 billion in 2002. In both business-to-business and business-to-consumer transactions e-commerce is rapidly becoming an accepted norm. Within Europe, growth is slower due to the later start and more innate conservatism of companies and individuals. Nevertheless, growth figures are impressive on any count. According to Logica, EU citizens, as distinct from businesses and corporations, will be spending more than £2.7 billion per year via e-commerce by the year 2000. Corporate usage of e-commerce is of a higher order of magnitude, as might be expected. In its annual study of the UK market, published in November 1997 (*Electronic Commerce Research Report*), KPMG Management Consulting looked at over 100 companies with a turnover above £200 million. According to the report, these companies expect online sales in the UK (not globally) to reach £350 billion by 2002.[48]

In *The Future of the Store* Field takes an in-depth look at the move by retailers away from looking at people as shoppers to looking at them as customers.[49] Retailers are moving to a customer-centric marketing model which recognises that the new consumer is demanding, informed, inquisitive, fickle, time-pressured, price-sensitive, willing to consider a variety of shopping and delivery channels, and has high expectations of customer service. The various loyalty schemes that are fast becoming ubiquitous are a response to the fact that consumers now have more choice than ever before. Electronic shopping will increase this choice many-fold and retailers will have to work even harder to raise spending and generate store traffic. Field looks in detail at consumer power and considers the agenda being set by consumers.

New national and European legislation is now curbing unchecked non-high-street retail development but, in the meantime, most of the major retailers have ambitious expansion plans for the next five years. Existing retail space is being developed, refurbished and recast in ways that will increase the diversity of retailing by both location and format. Field believes "the high street may need to be redefined and relocated but it will survive because of its ability to reinvent itself."[50]

His report goes on to look at globalisation, non-store retailers, the new value chain, return on investment and the casualties in each sector of the retail industry. The future? According to Field, the store will remain on the high street, in the shopping centre, the out-of-town retail park and on the petrol forecourt. However, in the future, it may appear as a concession within a large superstore, at motorway service stations, on an industrial estate, at the edge of a major tourist attraction or theme park, inside the warehouse of a large employer, in the middle of an abandoned airfield or at the edge of the M25. In short, "there is no single future for the store. New formats and themes will appear, new products will be invented, some old stores will carry on as before. There are any number of directions that a retailer can now take and still succeed or fail."[51]

The 'store' will not disappear, yet there is little agreement on how the store of the future will look, beyond acceptance that it will operate in a multi-channel market. Retailers may have to take a leaf out of the banks and building society's' book, and start to treat customers as accounts, offering them a range of retail services which span every single delivery channel.

Healey & Baker have analysed shopping centre development trends around the world. Their report shows that in Europe today, for example, there are over 55 million sq.m. of floorspace in shopping centres of over 5,000 sq.m.[52] Of this, shopping centres in France and the UK together account for approximately half, each having accumulated over 13 million sq.m. of retail floorspace, while developments in central and eastern Europe have been minimal. Approximately 7 million sq.m. of shopping centre floorspace is in the pipeline for completion up to the year 2000 across Europe. Of this, Germany has the largest amount of floorspace due to come on stream with approximately 2 million sq.m. The UK and Spain with approximately 1 million sq.m. each in the pipeline are set to see another phase of shopping centre development.

Healey & Baker look at the planning regulations in each country and conclude that they vary considerably in terms of the level of government to which developers must apply for planning permission. Most countries in Europe today have planning laws which attempt to protect traditional town centres from the perceived threat of out-of-town retailing competition. In the UK, the revised amendment to the Government's Policy Planning Guidance 6, which will only grant consent to out-of-town developments if they do not affect the 'vitality' and 'viability' of town centres, is compared to recent legislation in other European countries.

Healey & Baker's guide to rents of prime retail sites worldwide is one of the sources quoted in the *Travel Retailer International Yearbook*. The Yearbook highlights the most expensive retail site in the world as Hong Kong's Causeway Bay.[53] At $8,100 per sq. m., the cost of renting a shop on Causeway Bay is nearly 70% higher than that of the next most expensive site, New York's Fifth Avenue (Rockefeller Center to The Plaza), which costs $4,844. The third most expensive is Moscow's Trade House

Gum ($4,500), followed by the Champs Elysees in Paris ($3,127) and Orchard Road, Singapore ($2,850).

The survey covers rents obtainable in 168 prime retail sites in 30 countries. In the year to June 1996, retail rents rose in 41% of the sites examined. Factors fuelling growth include planning controls that strongly favour city centre retailing, limited availability of prime city centre space and the expansion plans of domestic and overseas retailers. Healey & Baker conclude that the structure of retailing continues to evolve at a dramatic pace, with many major groups expanding into new markets through franchising or joint ventures. New retail formats are being introduced across all markets, offering consumers, at times, a bewildering choice.

The *Yearbook* provides data on current developments and future trends in the $76 billion travel retailing market. There are four sections: 'View From the Top', which comprises exclusive interviews with 10 leading luxury goods executives on the performance and prospects of the travel-retail market; 'Retail Trends', which includes product trend predictions from more than 30 buyers, plus analyses from international property consultants Hillier Parker, Oncor International as well as Healey & Baker; 'Travel Trends' encompasses travel and tourism forecasts supplied by research bodies such as World Travel Organization, Generation DataBank, Airports Council International and the International Air Transport Association; 'Services' comprises three useful A-Z listings of contact details for trade exhibitions and events, associations and consultants and suppliers. The *Yearbook* is a practical aid to everyone in the travel-retail trade seeking to track the spending patterns and travel habits of the international shopper.

In July 1998 Safeway announced that it was opening stores on the forecourts of 100 BP filling stations. The move is an extension of a seven-store pilot joint venture between the two companies which started 18 months earlier. Ian Mumby, director of business development at Safeway, argues that shopping habits are changing, with shoppers increasingly combining a major shop at a superstore, where they stock up on bulky groceries, with more frequent forays to local stores to buy fresh food. The trend toward food shops on petrol forecourts has been rapidly taking hold. Tesco already operates Tesco Express stores at several of its own-brand petrol stations, and Shell has its Select shops. Budgens has two stores at Total petrol stations, six with BP and eight with Q8.

Budgens is also keen on the growing trend of putting small stand-alone supermarkets back into high streets. In 1997 it bought the 57-store 7-Eleven chain, renaming them b2 shops. Although four have been sold, 20 are being converted to small Budgens stores, with the remainder to be transformed into neighbourhood fresh food convenience outlets with the first opening in Pimlico in September 1998. Richard Hyman, chairman of retail analysts Verdict, said: "This is part of a growing trend. Contrary to popular perception, it is a myth that people only buy food in superstores. The neighbourhood market is worth £35 billion. It's enormous and fragmented and has been left behind by the big supermarkets." Hyman says that the oil companies are responding to a lack of profitability in fuel sales: "There is hardly any money in petrol retailing. There is more money in selling products from the shops."

Hyman says that while the supermarkets have reaped rewards in terms of profits as a result of spending the last decade developing huge stores, often out-of-town, they have now discovered that, thanks in part to a change of attitude by the planners, who are increasingly reluctant to permit such schemes, that the most lucrative sites have already been developed. That has made the stores look at what else they can do. "They have realised that people often don't want to do a massive shop," says Mr Hyman. "If you go to a big supermarket for two items, you are looking at parking in a huge car park and going to aisle 72 for one thing and aisle two for another. It becomes a mammoth expedition to buy a packet of fags, a paper and a pint of milk."

The £100 million Safeway/BP joint venture is expected to be rolled out over the next three to four years. The first of the new stores opened in Southend-on-Sea towards the end of 1998. Safeway expects the stores to generate sales of £700 million. Retail analysts have been unimpressed by the deal, and questioned whether it could make much difference to Safeway's languid performance. Bill Myers, an analyst at brokers Williams de Broe, said that the £700 million forecast would only be fulfilled if the chosen sites were particularly busy. He estimated that each one would have to sell 6 million litres of fuel a year. That compares to the average annual sales for a petrol station of 2 million litres.

One of the greatest problems facing retailers in the immediate future is the so-called 'millenium time bomb'. While this has a simple cause, its resolution is far more complex. Retailers, as a business sector, are particularly complacent about the dangers facing them as the millennium approaches. Part of the reason for this is that retail is seen as a 'people business'. However, the simple fact exists that computers are now all-pervasive and virtually every department of every business is dependent on them, either directly or indirectly. Most larger retailers do not just use tills, but complete electronic point-of-sale (EPoS) terminals that not only scan bar codes and calculate prices, but also monitor stock levels and automatically reorder products. These systems are frequently linked directly to both internal and external warehouse facilities, so that the product is automatically distributed to the shop floor and adequate supplies of fresh stock are arranged. At the warehouse, the same system is expanded to monitor demand from individual stores and to reorder from outside suppliers and wholesalers. Much of this activity is taken for granted, as it is transparent to the people carrying out the intermediate tasks of picking, loading and stacking products. The question that the senior management of retail organisations need to be asking is: "Are there systems in place that will enable the staff to continue working effectively in the event of a major system shutdown?" Many companies do have contingency plans to deal with shutdowns, but very few plans are designed to be able to sustain activity in the event of a prolonged shutdown.

In a recent FT Retail report Start and Phillips have examined the true nature of the Y2K problem as it relates to the retail industry, its causes and its effects, and identify the areas of greatest risk.[54] This is followed by a comprehensive description of the conditions of compliance being asked for by organisations such as banks and government departments. Their report also addresses the issues of recognised international standards, and how to verify that compliance has been met by all trading partners. Finally, they look at the project management for such an undertaking, and illustrate this with examples where available.

References

1   'It's four in the morning and Tesco tills are yawning', *Guardian*, 6/8/98.

2   Burke T and Shackleton J R, *Trouble in Store? UK Retailing in the 1990s* – London: Institute of Economic Affairs, 1996.

3   ibid.

4   Sherman P, The Next Big Thing, *Property Week*, 25 Jan 1996, p81-82.

5   Couch H, Centre Stage in Europe, *European Superstore Decisions*, Edition 3, 1996, p8-13.

6   Phillips Mike, *Retail Franchising: a Strategy for International Expansion* – London: FT Retail & Consumer Publishing, 1996.

7   NTC Publications, *British Shopper* – Henley-on-Thames, annual.

8   British Retail Consortium, *Annual Review* – London.

9   Humphries Gavin, *The Future for Airport Retailing: Opportunities and Threats in a Global Market* – London: FT Retail & Consumer Publishing, 1996.

10 Lamey Joanne, *Retail Internationalisation: Cross Border Strategies* – London: Pearson Professional, 1997.

11 Key Note, *Retailing in the UK* – Hampton, 1997.

12 Hendry Mike, *Improving Retail Efficiency through EDI: Managing the Supply Chain* – London: Pearson Professional, 1995.

13 Herman Gary, *IT and the Future of Retail: Integrating New Technologies and Processes* – London: FT Retail & Consumer Publishing, 1996.

14 Mintel *Efficient Consumer Response*, (Special Report) – London, 1997.

15 Mitchell A, *Efficient Consumer Response: a New Paradigm for the European FMCO Industry* – London: FT Retail & Consumer Publishing, 1997.

16 Institute of Grocery Distribution, *IT Trends in the Grocery Industry* – Watford, 1995.

17 Herman Gary, *The Impact of Information Technology: Globalisation and Customer Focus* – London: Financial Times Business Information, 1994.

18 Savage Tony, *Retail In-Store Systems: an In-Depth Critique of Proven Solutions* – Hove: RMDP, 1994.

19 Euromonitor, *European Retail Structures 2000* – London, 1995.

20 Mintel, *Financial Supermarkets* – London, 1996.

21 Mintel, *Customer Loyalty in Grocery Retailing* – London, 1995.

22 Mintel, *Grocery Retail Marketing* – London, 1997.

23 Mintel, *Customer Care in Retailing: Are we Being Served?* – London, 1996.

24 Mintel, *Customer Loyalty in Retailing* – London, 1996.

25 Rayner Sue, *Customer Loyalty Schemes: Effective Implementation and Management* – London: FT Retail & Consumer Publishing, 1996.

26 *Annual Review of Retailing*, Retail Trade Review no.38, June 1996 – London: Corporate Intelligence on Retailing.

27 Mintel, *Lifestage and Distribution Channels* – London, 1996.

28 Taylor Nelson AGB, *Grocery Shopper Profiles & Shopping Habits* – London, 1993.

29 Barnes Steve & Dadomo Simon, *Convenience Retailing – Profiting from Growth* – Watford: Institute of Grocery Distribution, 1996.

30 Phillips Mike, *UK Convenience Store Retailing: the Dynamics of Growth in a Key Market Sector* – London: FT Retail & Consumer Publishing, 1997.

31 Datamonitor, *Financial Services in the Retail Sector* – London, 1995.

32 Late-night shopping gains macho image, *Guardian*, 17/11/97.

33 Verdict, *Verdict on Retailing 2001* – London, 1997.

34 Corporate Intelligence on Retailing, *Retail Rankings* – London, 1997.

35 Newman Books, *Retail Directory of the UK* – London, 1998

36 Verdict, *Grocers & Supermarkets* – London, 1997.

37 Davies Dr Ross (ed.), *The Outlook for West European Retail: Regional Divergence and the Trend to Uniformity* – London: FT Retail & Consumer Publishing, 1996.

38 Smith Jeremy, *Category Killers in Europe: a Retail Format for the Future?* – London: Pearson Professional, 1995.

39 *Retail Pocket Book* – London: NTC Publications, 1997.

40 *British Shopping Centre Development Master List* – London: Hillier Parker, 1995.

41 *Sunday Trading – the Implications (1996: Two Years On)* – London: Healey & Baker, 1996.

42 Bracey-Gibbon Jonathan and Graham Richard, *The Future of Forecourt Retailing: a Roadside Retail Boom* – London: FT Retail & Consumer Publishing, 1997.

43 Market Assessment, *Forecourt Retailing* – London, 1995.

44 White Alexander, *Cross-border Retailing: Leaders, Losers and Prospects* – London: Pearson Professional, 1995.

45 Start Gerrard T and Phillips David, *Retail Transactions: the Future for Electronic Payment Systems* – London: FT Retail & Consumer Publishing, 1997.

46 Markham J, *The Future of Shopping: Traditional Patterns @nd Net Effects* – London: Macmillan, 1998.

47 Dedman Robert D, *Business Processes for Electronic Commerce: Profiting from the New Value Chains* – London: FT Media & Telecoms, 1998.

48 KPMG Management Consulting, *Electronic Commerce Research Report* – London, 1997.

49 Field Christopher, *The Future of the Store: New Formats and Channels for a Changing Retail Environment* – London: FT Retail & Consumer Publishing, 1997.

50 ibid.

51 ibid.

52 Healey & Baker, *Main Streets Across the World* – London, 1996.

53 *Travel Retailer International Yearbook* – London: Raven Fox, 1997.

54 Start Gerard T and Phillips D, *Retail and the Millenium Time Bomb : a Survival Guide* – London: FT Retail & Consumer, 1998.

4 Online Shopping for All: the Future?

Datamonitor, the research firm, estimated recently that European online retail shopping will grow from just $108 million in 1997 to reach $4.65 billion by 2002. The US Commerce Department's recently released report on 'The Emerging Digital Economy' noted that "Internet commerce is growing fastest among businesses – it is used for co-ordination between the purchasing operations of a company and its suppliers; the logistics planners in a company and the transportation companies that warehouse and move its produce; the sales organisations and the wholesalers or retailers that sell its products; and the consumer services and maintenance operations and the company's final customers." As a result, while consumer-related e-commerce grabs most of the headlines, Price Waterhouse, in its' latest annual technology forecast, says that the real growth is occuring in business-to-business e-commerce. Price Waterhouse reckons that business-to-business e-commerce doubled every six months between 1996 and 1997 and will accelerate to double every three or four months during 1998. By 2002 Price Waterhouse estimates that the value of goods and services traded on the World Wide Web will be $434 billion. Of this, $94 billion will be consumer purchases but the vast bulk will be business to and from companies.

Among the sectors affected by this surge in e-commerce are:

Financial Services: nearly half of the trades executed by Charles Schwab, America's largest discount brokerage house, were conducted online during the first three months of 1998. That compared with one-third in the same period of 1997. Overall, nearly 5 million people traded stocks via the Internet in 1997 and the number is expected to reach 10-16 million by 2000.

Travel: in 1996, independent travel agents handled 80% of US airline reservations. Today, their share is down to 52% as airlines deal directly with travellers over the telephone or via web sites.

Computer hardware: Dell Computer now generates sales of more than $4 million a day from its web site, up from $1 million a day in 1997. Meanwhile, 41% of Cisco's sales are now generated over the Internet and web sales are running at an annual rate of over $3.6 billion.

Booksellers: Amazon.com, the first online book seller, had web site sales of $148m in 1997, up 838% from 1996. Amazon is still making losses, but the 2 million people who visited Amazon's online book store in December 1997 – with more than 1.5 million placing an order – have traditional booksellers worried. The largest bookshops may carry 150,000 titles while online there is a choice of 2.5 million.

It seems that everywhere you turn there is 'Net-talk'. Most commentators are making predictions on the growth of the Internet and the potential of online shopping. Below are a selection of recent opinions:

* Net advertising topped $350 million in the first three months of 1998, up 171% from the same period in 1997 (*Coopers and Lybrand*).

* between May 1997 and May 1998, Internet users increased by 53 to 92 million. During the same period, Web commerce rose 205% to $2.3 billion (*IDC Internet Commerce Market Model*).

* nearly one-third of online homes made a purchase on the Net in the first six months of 1998. Those who didn't buy online still used the Net to make purchasing decisions (*Odyssey*).

* the value of online purchases by US households in 1997 reached $511 million, and is expected to jump to $1.6 billion by 2001 (*Piper Jaffray*).

* US businesses will have traded an estimated $17 billion in goods and services over the Net by the end of 1998 (Table 4.1), a lot of this business-to-business commerce and services conducted by the world's leading conglomerates (*Forrester Research*).

* the number of Web sites profitable by the end of 1997 rose to 46%, up from 30% the previous year (*Activmedia*).

* conducting business on the Net results in cost savings of 5-10% of sales – savings that can, but not necessarily will, be passed on to consumers (*Business Week Poll*).

* Europe's online population is expected to grow to a modest 13% between now and 2001. This compares dismally to a US increase to 40% in the same time period (*Forrester*).

- despite Europe's greater population, it will trail way behind the US in the number of people online by 2001. Europe is expected to have 53.2 million online users, the US 98 million users (*Forrester*).

- E-commerce is expected to be at least three times more important to business in the US as it is to Europe (*Forrester*).

Table 4.1 Internet Commerce Between Businesses in the US ($bn)

	1997	1998	1999	2000	2001	2002
Internet commerce (all business-to-business)	8	17	41	105	183	327
Manufacturing	3	8	17	41	68	116
Wholesale/business retail	2	6	18	48	89	168
Utilities	2	2	3	5	7	10
Services	1	1	3	11	19	33

(**Source**: Forrester Research)

No company worth its salt wants to miss out on the greatest retailing opportunity of the 20th century. In this final section of the review we look at the attempts made by some of the major retailers to expand their role in the marketplace of the future.

In July 1998 Waitrose launched a service which allows customers to do their weekly shop without leaving the workplace. It is the latest in a series of experiments by the supermarket groups in remote ordering and delivery. The service has already signed up British Airways' new head office at Harmondsworth and is talking to BT, the BBC, Nationwide building society and Microsoft, whose internet technology is used in the system. Dubbed Waitrose@work, the new operation has been developed in conjunction with the computer company ICL, whose Reading head office has been used as a test site over the past year.

The Waitrose service is based on ICL's intranet technology, which must be installed before workers can shop from their desks. The office must also be near a Waitrose store – all of which are in the south of England – and have car parking for staff so they can take the shopping home after work. Then workers can order through their personal computers from the full range of products in the local store. The orders are faxed by ICL to the relevant store and assembled by store staff. Delivery, which is free for orders of more than £5 will be by lunchtime for orders placed by 9.30am, or in the evening.

Keith Todd, ICL's chief executive, says that the new venture is a clear example of how technology could change people's lives. "It's what I call the Martini effect – any time, any place, any where", he said. Jenny Sharp, head of global services at BA, says becoming Waitrose's first customer was part of the airline's attempt to introduce new ways of working at its new headquarters. "Challenges in life are getting tougher, both in people's work and domestic lives. We believe very, very strongly that a good employer should assist staff in meeting those challenges," she said. "If we can take the hassle and stress out of people's lives they will be much more productive."

Mark Price, Waitrose marketing director, claimed the cost to employers of setting up the system would be "minimal". He said the operation overcame problems which have been experienced with Internet-based systems, especially the slowness of placing orders and the limited product range on some services. Mr Price also pointed out delivery to offices was more viable than home delivery, and more practical for many workers because they did not have to specify a time when they would be at home to receive the shopping. The service is not necessarily limited to large employers, since smaller companies sharing a business park could club together to subscribe.

Home Shopping: How the Supermarkets Line Up
(as at 11/7/98)

Safeway   Trial of *Collect'n'go* at Basingstoke store, for holders of the ABC card; full range of products; order by phone or fax; no home delivery; collection from store within 2-hour time slots on the next day.

Asda   Aims to use remote shopping in areas where it does not have stores; will deliver within a six-mile radius of depots; customers will order by phone or fax from a reduced range of 5,000 lines; delivery to cost £3.50, within a 2-hour time slot, possibly on the same day.

Sainsbury's Orderline being extended from seven to 32 stores; orders by phone, fax, internet; full range of products; delivery £5 to home (next day), £3.50 if collected from store; 2-hour time window.

Somerfield Home delivery at 30 stores, being extended to 130; phone or fax ordering from limited catalogue; free if more than £25 and within 3 mile radius of store.

Tesco 32 stores offering home-shopping in London, 1 in Leeds; full range; order by internet, phone, fax, CD-rom; £5 charge for delivery within 2-hour time slot, possibly same day.

Home delivery services could capture £8 billion of supermarket and grocery spending a year, prompting a wave of difficulties for Britain's biggest food chains, according to a recent survey from the property specialists Healey & Baker. The survey suggests that about 16% of the entire grocery spend could transfer to home delivery or the "drive thru" format within the next few years. That could make weekly visits to the supermarket a thing of the past for many families. But a lower rate of shop usage for the big food groups such as Tesco and Sainsbury's would have serious consequences and would almost inevitably fuel fresh competition. John Strachan, head of retail at Healey & Baker, said: "The received wisdom of the 1990s is that supermarkets compete for customers through price. Our survey shows that shoppers are more interested in quality and service. The demand for delivery and collection services follows on from this."

Healey & Baker argue that electronic ordering and home delivery can provide what shoppers want and give retailers the chance to reduce operating costs. But most supermarket chains would suffer if the use of their expensive shops were to be reduced. And it has been suggested that once the link between the supermarket, as provider of everything, and the shopper has been broken there could be a swing back to traditional high street outlets such as butchers and green grocers. The study indicates that more than one in five shoppers surveyed would be interested in a home delivery service, estimated to be worth about £8 billion of spending a year. About 11% – mainly families and high earners – also expressed interest in a "drive thru" system, where they would collect goods which have already been ordered, rather like the system operated by some fast food outlets.

Britain does believe the hype. More than 250,000 people are shopping on-line. These are the findings of a study carried out by NOP Research Group. NOP estimate that consumers bitten by the techno-bug will trigger on-line shopping transactions totalling more than £1 billion a year. The most popular purchases are computer hardware and software products, but books, CDs, travel tickets and holidays are also pulling in the buyers. General surfing on the the Net is also on the increase – more than four million people tried using it during 1997. But despite such optimism, many consumers are still nervous about the lack of security involved in carrying out financial transactions on-line. In an effort to dispel such fears, AT&T plans to develop a solution which will make "micropayments" – under £10 – commercially viable on the World Wide Web. Using the Mondex electronic cash platform, customers will soon be able to transfer cash electronically and securely between smartcards. Initially, AT&T will pilot the scheme with selected on-line merchants, but expects to expand in 1998/99.

Why will consumers bother with shopping online? Mastercard International sponsored a consumer survey, conducted by Yankelovich Partners, to determine why consumers are increasingly choosing to shop from their homes. They surveyed 502 shoppers ranging from traditional shoppers to TV shoppers to computer shoppers. They found several interesting reasons based on their research. These were *safety* (75% of all respondents claimed that they no longer felt safe shopping in malls); *service* (62% of the respondents claimed that they had left a store because there had not been a sales clerk available); *knowledge* (most consumers felt that the sales representatives simply were not knowledgeable about the products that they sell); and *convenience* (over half the respondents to the survey stated that they would be willing to pay a little more for products if the consumer would be able to purchase them in more timely fashion). Although the survey was conducted in the United States, to a lesser extent these reasons also hold good for the UK. Retail industry forecasters predict that as many as 40% of all shoppers will try home shopping in the next two years and 15% may become home shopping regulars. But, the promised boom in sales over the next ten years will not happen until the shopping mediums become interactive. People would rather actively shop than passively watch TV.

An 'intelligent agent' may be the thing that persuades shoppers away from the high street and on to their home computer. Imagine a TV dial with 500 channels, 400 of which sell everything from wristwatches and hiking boots to accounting software and consulting help. We do not have to imagine all that much if we look at the shopping networks and malls in their infancy on the Internet. If a shopper were looking for a particular type of product, they would give up in frustration long before they found what they needed, not to mention being able to comparison shop. Intelligent agents might be the answer to this problem. These are programs that search for things based on the specifications that are given to it. The agent may be told to look for a red turtle neck, size medium, in the price range £15-20. The intelligent agent would then search through catalogues and the inventory of vendors and give the list back to the consumer.

This program would solve several problems. First of all, it would allow the consumer to comparison shop fairly easily. The consumer would get all of the items that fit the specifications and can then choose from the possibilities which product would best suit their needs. Secondly, intelligent agents offer a solution to one of the greatest problems of the Internet: the overwhelming amount of information. This information is wonderful, but it also gets in the way when searching for something specific. Many of the vendor's catalogues and cyber-malls offer search capabilities (the Internet Shopping Network has a good one), but they are confined to a particular mall or vendor. The breadth that is necessary to sufficiently comparison shop is simply not found in one location.

The Oxford Institute of Retail Management (OXIRM) is conducting ongoing research into the growth of electronic commerce, specifically via the Internet. In his report on the progress made so far, Reynolds considers the variation in European opportunities which Internet connectivity affords, before reviewing progress in two comparative sectors: the activity of major conventional mail order companies and that of grocery retailers worldwide.[1]

Reynolds cites the story of Yorkshire butcher Jack Scaife, who has become a global business as a consequence of £1,000 spent on developing a web site within the 'Classic England' online shopping mall. Scaife's success has been well-documented. Ten months after setting up the service, some 20% of the company's business – half from outside the UK – comes through the net. Black pudding may not have been the product which commentators had in mind when talking about the potential for small businesses to compete more easily within a global market place. Nevertheless, it represents a telling example of one of the ways in which a new marketing channel such as the Internet can open up business opportunities and permit a levelling out of the playing field for SMEs, amongst others. Such channels, however, are not without their risks but, arguably, the risks are greater for MNCs and large national corporations than for their smaller brethren.

In his first case study, Reynolds examines electronic mail order. Existing mail order and direct marketing operators start with established strengths in dealing with an Internet route to market in that they are already non-store based. Recent research undertaken by PIRA International claims that "the mail order companies are laying the foundations for viable one-to-one shopping services ... and are way ahead of conventional retailers when it comes to establishing an online ordering system on the Internet." A further strength of many mail order houses rests in their increasingly international presence. This positions them well to take advantage of the global nature of the Internet medium.

Nearly all the major players in the established mail order sector have developed an online presence. Quelle sees its web site as the natural development of an involvement with online dating back to 1979 and the German *Bildschirmtext* videotex service. Global market leader Otto Versand claims sales via new media to be running at over $200 million in 1996. The company's web site was begun in late 1995 and offers the entire product portfolio. This is nothing exceptional. What sets these sites apart from the competition, however, is the scale of the support operation. The continuing preoccupation with the 'catalogue' has led to the growth of a number of metasites offering a buyer's guide to mail order catalogues. 'Buyer's Index' is a bespoke search engine launched in November 1996. It offers access to over 8,000 listed mail order companies and over 19 million products. Its mission, to "help mail order buyers find the best suppliers on or off the net."

Reynolds looks to online grocery retailing for the second case study in his article. He feels we have to look to the US in order to get some sense of what an emerging competitive market could look like. The consumer in the Boston market, for example, has up to seven electronic grocery merchants to choose from. All have their different attributes, brands and positioning. A personal shopper assistant (intelligent agent) helps with difficult-to-find items. As far as Europe is concerned, online grocery retailing is relatively piecemeal. In the UK, for example, Tesco Direct has received the most recent press attention. However, despite featuring in the Marketing Society IT Awards for 1998, the press, in particular the *Sunday Times*, has recently sought to demonstrate that the Tesco home shopping initiative largely consists of string and sealing wax behind the PC interface. The newspaper suggests that at Tesco Direct's Dryburgh, Dundee, HQ, 'cyberspace meets elbow grease.' Reynolds states that those with any serious knowledge of the way retailing works would find this unsurprising. Off-shelf picking of grocery goods is, of course, astronomically expensive for the large retailers. Whilst acceptable during experimentation or trial periods, it is inconceivable that a fully-commercial roll-out could operate profitably on this basis.

A halfway house has been the growth of back-of-store picking operations within continental Europe, although some commentators suggest that UK-based operators are unlikely to have the space. Ian O'Reilly of Tesco comments: "One of the key drivers of home shopping in terms of profitability is pick-up productivity. One of the ways we can get better pick-up productivity is through simple, semi-automated picking. Our ambition will be when you send in your Internet order, it goes untouched by human hand all the way down to the picking trolley." The company has been reported to be on the point of re-launching its web site, incorporating an expansion of the home shopping facilities available only in a comprehensive way to carefully delimited catchments around 11 stores.

Tesco's home shopping service appears to have its supporters as well as its critics: 96% of those using the service would recommend it to others; only 15% of those who had tried stopped using it by the end of 1997. In the UK, competitors include Sainsbury's, with plans announced in April 1998 to expand its operation, Orderline, to over 32 stores and 4 million customers nationwide. Insight Research suggests that the competitors are really the small specialist home shopping operators, like Food Ferry, Flanagans and Teleshop, the recently floated Asda spin-off. However, such SME activity is risky: Teleshop was forecast to lose £234,000 before tax on £14.4 million turnover in the year ending March 1998.

The enthusiasm of IT supplier companies to embrace electronic commerce has led many to be at the forefront of the grocery trials. Microsoft, HP, IBM, ICL, Oracle and Cap Gemini have all provided employees to be guinea-pigs for office shopping rather than home shopping experiments. ICL's experience with Waitrose has proved instructive. It proved difficult to attract even IT-literate males to use the ordering service and so the ICL 'family day' was used as a means of signing up spouses. The concept has been adapted by the Svenska Coop and by a supermarket chain in the Paris area for supplying physically remote office parks.

Verdict is on record as suggesting that electronic commerce is not likely to have a major impact on the grocery sector in the foreseeable future and will, in any case not account for more than 5% of food sales within the UK over the next ten years. Given that 5% of UK food sales is equivalent to the turnover of Kwik Save at around £3bn, perhaps this represents a new definition of the word 'cautious' by Verdict.

Reynolds concludes his article by suggesting two basic positioning strategies for retailers on the Internet: informational or transactional, which seek to *complement* or *substitute* for conventional routes to the consumer.

Online Digital Payments (ODP) represents the next step in the development of the Internet. ODP will enable the Internet to develop from an information network into a commercial network. According to Datamonitor we will look back on 1996–97 as the period when the combined efforts of IT companies, financial institutions and retailers, accompanied by a shift in consumer attituides towards online shopping, prepared the way for creating a "critical mass of transactions that will kick start market growth."[2]

The report predicts that the online shopping market will grow at an average 100% annually from now until the year 2002. Based on the analysis of the market conditions in 1996–97 the consumer online shopping market will be worth $16bn. The US and European markets will be worth $12.5 billion and $3.5 billion respectively. The introduction of micropayments, small-value payments and credit card based ODPs will be the key factors in producing this rate of growth.

The key findings of Datamonitor's report conclude that:

- By 2002, 95% of payments used in US Internet shopping and 75% of European transactions will be settled online using credit/debit cards.

- In early 1999, smartcards will be introduced into the European online shopping market as the price of smartcard readers falls. By 2002, 7% of online transactions in Europe, and 2% in the US will be completed using smartcards.

- Electronic cash products will lose market share to credit/debit cards and smartcard payments from the middle of 1998 onwards.

- In 1999 micropayments will come "on-stream". By 2002, micropayments will account for up to 12% of online transactions in the US and 8% in Europe.

- By 2002, 38 million households in Europe will have Internet access, 5 million less than the US. The US Internet market will mature gradually during 1998–2000 whilst the European market will continue its rapid growth.

- During 1996–97 more Europeans have become aware of the Internet, and more users have become willing to pay for Internet access from their homes rather than using office locations.

Are retailers and consumers ready for E-cash, electronic wallets and cyber cash? The spectacular growth figures for ODP should be kept in perspective. Verdict Research valued online retailing in the UK at £1 million as compared to £160 billion for total retailing in 1997. Clearly there is still a way to go before Internet retailing makes serious inroads into the traditional spending habits of the consumer. The current problems of Internet shopping have yet to be overcome, including the time taken to connect to sites, the connection costs themselves and the simple fact that Internet shopping is still hampered by the low use of the Internet at home. British Telecom estimates that there are only about 300,000 homes in the UK with personal computers connected to the Internet. The majority of Internet users are work based and shopping is not one of their priorities.

A report by OXIRM highlighted the main anxieties expressed by retailers. The top four concerns were: too few users, an inappropriate market segment, inadequate financial security, and lack of delivery infrastructure. However, the report felt that these concerns were misplaced. The concern over payment sysytems for example was a short-term one, "being largely a technical debate driven by psychological overtones in terms of perceived consumer behaviour."

Much of the reporting on the development of the Internet as a shopping medium is based on supposition and prediction. As Chris Talbot, Research Associate at OXIRM, says, "the fact remains that nobody is entirely certain as to what constitutes the current volume of trade, let alone what it will be in four years time. Some commentators believe it has been over-hyped, others believe that the market has been underestimated. Clearly ODP will be the most significant factor in transforming the Internet from an information channel to transactional channel but how soon ODP will make a significant impact on Internet sales is really anyone's guess."

Market Assessment (MAPS) produced one of the first reports to look at the changing face of the financial services industry in the light of technological advances.[3] The impact of new technology has meant that traditional financial institutions have had to find new means of serving their customers in order to survive. The appeal of telephone banking to customers is that they can deal with their financial affairs at a time that suits them without leaving the office or home. This concept appeals particularly to those who are 'resource rich and time poor.'

Electronic retailing is seen as a means of diversifying and promoting economies of scale, particularly in view of slower sales in the high street. The majority of retailers may well end up with dual channels of distribution – stores or branches and an electronic form whether it be via the TV/PC or telephone. However, it is certain that the banks have yet to pronounce definitively on the future of the high street branch. Banks are trying to integrate electronic retailing with branch operations so that their customers can choose the most appropriate channel to deal with them. MAPS conclude that there is nothing to support the prediction that banks will one day move out of branch banking. Technology will enable them to increase the number of channels to reach customers, not narrow them.

In the past five years home shopping has increased greatly and looks set to continue to do so. By the turn of the century it will be running at more than twice the level of 1990. Direct banking will exhibit even greater growth rates, with the telephone the cornerstone of the growth, and by the year 2000 MAPS forecasts that just under a third of accounts will be operated away from the bank branch. This growth will be aided by consumer's increased movement away from cash purchases to purchases on plastic.

Essinger has looked at the major trends in specific types of virtual financial services such as ATM's, EFTPoS, remote banking and smart cards.[4] These trends are summarised in general terms, along with a look at other probable key future trends in virtualisation. He identifies the following trends:-

- increasing customer demand for virtual financial services
- institutions will continue to implement virtual financial services, and the pace of implementation will quicken
- virtual infrastructure will increasingly unify and become nationwide
- virtual networks will become increasingly international
- technology used in operating virtual financial services will become increasingly fast and powerful
- increases in the numbers of market participants will lead to a corresponding increase in the number of mergers of these organisations, and to shake-outs
- increasing possibilities will occur for eliminating the institution from the virtual transaction process entirely
- the user interface for virtual financial services will become increasingly virtual.

Essinger feels the role of the Internet in the development of virtual financial services is not straightforward. While the Internet is certainly an extremely useful way of obtaining a wide range of information, including details of financial products and services offered by institutions, Essinger believes its potential as a delivery agent for virtual financial services is – at least at present – severely restricted by the following factors:

- in its current form it is not specifically designed for the rapid, interactive transactions that customers require in dealing with their institutions by virtual means

- it is not readily secure. Internet information is available to all browsers. Software is becoming available to improve Internet security, but linking this to a customer-specific authorisation system is difficult, and rather militates against the 'open to all' idea of the Internet

- the special computer equipment required in order for the user to connect to the Internet is expensive and, unless the price for this equipment comes down dramatically, would be regarded as prohibitive by the families who are for most institutions the prime targets for their virtual financial services

- obtaining access to Internet-delivered information is slow. Gaining access usually takes on average from about half a minute to several minutes. These kind of access speeds greatly restrict the usefulness of the Internet as a delivery channel for virtual financial services

- connections to the Internet are frequently broken due to high volumes of traffic. Users of Internet-delivered virtual financial services would find broken connections extremely frustrating and annoying.

These problems may be solved in the future, but, Essinger believes, for the time being they remain as difficulties which severely restrict the usefulness of the Internet. As far as its potential for delivering virtual financial services is concerned the Internet may turn out to have been overhyped. Virtual financial services, though, will in all probability remain the dominant phenomenon in the retail banking industry.

In the second edition of Fletcher's analysis of the electronic commerce market he concentrates primarily on the influence of the Internet on 'electronic data interchange (EDI)'.[5] In 1996 the term 'electronic commerce' came to mean Internet-based commerce as well as that carried out by EDI. Various estimates have placed the value of EC-based trade at US$4 billion for 1997 rising to US$200 billion in 2000. However, it is important to determine the actual measure – these figures generally apply to sales made online, not transaction values which will be much higher.

Essentially electronic commerce provides two functions: a marketplace where products can be bought and paid for, and a communications system which substitutes existing financial and commercial processes such as banking. Electronic commerce relies on the substitution of existing activities by electronic means. Thus we see that the US$60 billion a year spent on catalogue production and distribution in the USA is a target for electronic catalogue mechanisms. Smartcards which are connected online can become a procurement mechanism. The 500 million credit cards and 300 million debit cards can be enabled for online usage if a protocol is established. Fletcher's report looks at the different models required in order to understand the application of electronic commerce.

The report also predicts the effect of the Internet on the EDI market, although the effect is still too early to discern in reality. The core EDI business is worth some US$1 billion per year, comprising revenues from subscription, traffic, mailboxes and connections. Various government programmes aimed at small businesses could potentially expand that value by 50%. Fletcher believes that these companies, and the conventional new subscribers generated, will preferentially opt to implement EDI by Internet, for reasons of cost and ease. The key factor for small companies is the development of web-based EDI messaging. Whilst the market will expand above the normal 20% per year growth experienced hitherto, the value per subscriber will fall due to the lower cost of implementation.

Fletcher looks at the crucial issue of security in electronic commerce. The global connectivity of the Internet enables online ordering and payment. The many existing forms of payment scheme (cheque, bank transfer, credit card) can be implemented electronically once a public key infrastructure (PKI) system is in place. Beyond that, new forms of payment become possible, such as the stored value card, electronic cash and electronic wallets and anonymous payments (true cash). Many pilots are currently running, but there is little indication of winners and losers yet. It seems likely that governments and financial institutions will have a big say in the use of preferred systems, but as always with the Internet, this cannot be assumed.

Despite the fact that businesses have been leaping onto the Internet at record rates, few have mastered the art of electronic commerce. Companies are looking for the right mix of tools and technology to push virtual retailing to a new level. At the Electronic Commerce Conference in Newport Beach, California, in 1996, more than 200 Internet experts gathered to share their ideas about virtual retailing.[6] Their analysis: a mixture of high-tech tools and non-traditional approaches combined with old fashioned customer service will be the key to making sales on the Net.

Bourne cites the four critical elements of successful virtual retail as suggested by Tennenbaum, the founder of CommerceNet:

1. Offer truly useful products and services that exploit the medium and offer real value.
2. Develop virtual retail objectives that fit your company's mission.
3. Look for new ways of doing business.
4. Offer secured transactions.

At the same Conference the President of Netscape claimed that the Net will be a place of commerce when it can accomplish three things:

1. Reach a state where it is ubiquitous.
2. Be affordable (it was noted that in 1920 it cost $30 to make a cross-country long-distance phone call).
3. Be useful and offer utility.

The uses and advantages of digital media and the market potential of the online channel have been considered by Thompson in a recent FT report.[7] He provides a general background to the online economics of the channel and demonstrates how convergence in the global telecoms infrastructure is helping to bring down the costs of information access and transmission. There is an up-to-date analysis of the online channel, its likely evolution, and the activities of many of the major technology suppliers, infrastructure owners and content providers in a global context. Authoritative surveys and sources are used to provide a timely, accurate snapshot of the current state of the online channel, its likely development in the foreseeable future and potential investment opportunities.

The market research publisher Key Note has valued the UK home shopping industry at around £8.45 billion in 1996, accounting for 5.1% of total retail sales.[8] The market is divided into three main areas: general mail order, direct marketing and direct selling. In their report Key Note concentrate on these areas but also look at electronic home shopping, which it expects to become increasingly important. The potential for growth in electronic retailing is linked to the rise in the number of consumers with access to communications technology such as modems and PCs, knowledge of how to use them, and a growing awareness of electronic shopping opportunities, such as sites on the Internet and other computer communications. A medium such as CD-ROMs will also be utilised increasingly by both consumers and retailers for the display and purchasing of goods. The wider number of cable, terrestial and non-terrestial TV stations is also likely to result in an increase in the number of TV shopping channels of the type pioneered in the UK by QVC. In the medium to long term, electronic shopping is likely to grow dramatically, encouraged by increased consumer access to appropriate technology, as well as wider acceptance and trust in electronic transfer of both orders and monies. At the moment, this area tends to be more supplier than consumer focused, but the benefits and potential of electronic shopping will encourage greater and greater use as the millenium approaches. Key Note forecasts that the overall home shopping market will grow by 24.9% between 1996 and 2001 to £10.55 billion.

Global growth of home shopping channels is finally about to take off. At present there are 70 projects in various stages of development. By the end of the decade there will be over 500 shopping channels. Every national telecom, media company, mail order and retailer is developing multi-media departments and investigating the practicality and profitability of home shopping.

Verdict Research have dismissed claims by computer companies that the world's shoppers will one day be using the Internet rather than the high street or shopping centre to buy festive items i.e. Christmas shopping.[9] Whilst computer companies have hyped the future benefits of the Internet to advertisers and retailers, analysts at Verdict predict the web will really satisfy only young male "techies"! Research manager Clive Vaughan said: "It is too early to call the future for the Internet. Retail is still at the experimental stage, but we think it will only ever be really popular with young men who are computer fanatics. The Net is not suited for young women with kids at home. They want to get out of the house. Why would they want to be in front of a TV? High street shops will always be the most popular sales channel because people will always want to see, feel and try the goods they buy. Another problem is that delivery of goods from Internet purchases is a real pain. If you order anything too big for the letterbox, you have to wait in for it to be delivered. In the time you waste sitting around waiting, you could have been down to the shops and bought the goods yourself." Verdict goes on to claim that the Internet will only be big for sales of computer hardware, music, films and books – and perhaps, in time, financial services. Security, especially on credit card sales, was still perceived by many respondents as a major problem.

Christopher Field has taken an in-depth look at the impact of the Internet on retailing and the future prospects of retailing as a whole. Some of his key findings are as follows:

"...the retail world of the future is both global and local. The globalisation of the market is threatening virtually all retailers' traditional customer franchise – consumers are no longer being served solely by the high street store but by a variety of physical and remote channels. In response, retailers are trying to 'localise', to move from mass marketing to mass customisation, using these new channels. The global is here.

- The convergence of computing, communications and information is altering the way consumers select retailers and choose, order and pay for goods, with growing numbers plugging into the new interactive technologies on the so-called information superhighway – one strand of which is the Internet.

- The Internet is becoming the first global public computer network that is accessible to all, easy to use and inexpensive. It is anticipated that this democracy of access will attract a mass audience, one that is prepared to undertake commercial transactions electronically. There are currently about 30 million people accessing the Internet. By 2000 this is forecast to grow to 52 million, with some estimates of over 100 million.

- Networks such as the Internet present tantalising opportunities for retailers to find competitive advantage, exploit new markets unreachable by traditional methods, achieve high customer retention rates and engage in cross-selling, all at reduced operating and distribution costs. Tantalising, but as yet achieved by only a handful of retailers. And yet Microsoft's Bill Gates and others say that the Internet cannot be ignored: "the Internet is a tidal wave. It will wash over the computer industry and many others, drowning those who don't learn to swim in its waves." It is this vision of drowning while competitors swim profitably in the waves that is behind many of the 'me-too' Web sites that are springing up.

- Estimates for the value of business passing over the Net vary from $10 billion to $100 billion. The broad definition of 'business' as any exchange of information whether paid for on-line or at some later date, is not helpful for retailers: Digital alone claims to sell over $3 billion a year worth of software and services. Non-business consumers account for about 10% of Internet users and a value of £500 million a year, a tiny amount compared to all remote shopping of $100 billion. Estimates suggest that between 5% and 7% of existing shopping from physical stores will be electronic by 2005.

- It will be several years before meaningful figures are available that companies can bank on. This is one reason why most companies are taking a 'softly softly' approach to the Net, testing the water in order to find out who is interested before backing it up with integrated fulfilment and payment infrastructures.

- With the emergence of the Internet as a commercial platform, the remote relationships that retailers are attempting to manage on the telephone through automated call centres and integrated customer files will be complemented by intercomputer relationships. Using the Internet, the customer will take more control of the relationship in deciding how products and services will be designed, presented and managed. Research is required into how consumers act on the Internet, accepting that the physical retail environment can only be partially reproduced through virtual shopping malls.

- According to one study undertaken at the end of 1995, 19% of US consumers had already tapped into the Internet and a further 12% said they planned to in 1996. Of the current users, 27% had bought something.

- The Internet is only one medium for electronic commerce. Other forms of remote shopping are competing aggressively with the Internet, and in some cases are merging with it to create hybrid forms. Alongside their interest in the Internet, some medium and large retailers are therefore experimenting with in-store and public multimedia kiosks, loyalty and database marketing, interactive TV and cable/satellite/telephone-connected TV home shopping that may or may not use the Internet.

- The suitability of certain goods and services for Internet commerce is under debate. While a healthy traffic in software, music products and flowers already exists, retailers are also concerned to discover whether fresh foods can be successfully ordered and delivered in an Internet transaction, or whether goods that traditionally need to be seen, touched or even tested can be sold or simply promoted.

- Taken in isolation from electronic commerce as a whole, the prospects for Internet shopping do not look strong enough to justify the time and resources that retailers are committing to it. However, in the wider context of electronic commerce and financial services, the Internet will be at the forefront of all the technologies and channels that are being built for remote commerce.

- The Internet was never conceived as a commercial channel and the necessary requirements for fast, secure commerce will be difficult to patch on to the existing network, not least because the open configuration of the Internet does not lend itself to electronic payments.

- In five years' time the Internet will start to force some retailers to look again at exactly what businesses they are in. By a narrow definition, retailers are in the business of upmarket warehousing. The value they add is in presentation, design, location and advice, all benefits that can be replicated and often enhanced in cyberspace. Some retailers will therefore shift their distribution to remote channels and either reduce or terminate their high street presence. Equally, new retailers that started life on the Internet will seek a physical high street presence to grow their brand presence.

- As more and more non-retailers become retailers on the Net, the high street store will undergo changes. The sections of stores where consumers spend most of their time are fresh food at one end and drink at the other. All the sections in between may fall victim to home delivery. The role of the large, edge and out-of-town store will be thrown into doubt."[10]

In an article in *Retail World* Charles reports on a study by KPMG on the current and potential use of the Internet by retailers across Europe. He quotes the number of computers connected to the Internet worldwide as having doubled during 1995 to 9.4 million. With a single computer supporting up to a thousand users, it is estimated that up to 30 million users are connected worldwide. Whilst the US still dominates, Europe now has some 23% of connectivity. The user profile represents some previously hard-to-reach but very desirable market segments, comprising people with relatively high incomes and educational levels as well as "innovative, stimulation-seeking and fashionable young people."[11] The increasing popularity of the Internet is leading some observers to suggest that the ultimate teleshopping vehicle has arrived, at last.

Despite the growth in the number of people connected to the Internet and the attractions of the audience, the KPMG's study argues that retailers must be wary of embracing this electronic channel simply because others are. Retailers seeking to invest in Internet ventures need to devote as much, if not more, care and attention to researching and understanding the market, to the design and crafting of their offers and to their skills and capabilities in delivering the offer as they would in the development of more conventional physical storefronts. In particular, European retailers need to be aware of:

- the very different characteristics and requirements of electronic channels to market

- the very varied picture of experience, barriers and opportunities across Europe

- the potentially wide range of positioning opportunities available.

An important consideration for retailers is whether their marketing assets are directly transferable to an electronic channel. They must then decide whether an Internet presence is to be purely international or transactional in nature and as a consequence determine their positioning strategy. Although the UK currently has over 300 retail sites on the WWW, many of these retailers have chosen a relatively passive presence.

There are a number of obstacles to effective Internet usage, some of which are short term and will be overcome through technological advances and changes in consumer attitudes. However, the main strategic concerns highlighted by the study are:

- problems associated with the transferability of the brands into electronic channels

- the suitability of distribution networks as the Internet relies on one-to-one distribution channels which may be at variance with conventional retail cost structures

- global exposure and the removal of territorial boundaries

- the changing relationship between suppliers and retailers as the retailer's conventional role as an intermediary becomes more difficult to justify.

In the UK, more than 25% of households currently own a PC and domestic Internet penetration is estimated to be as high as 6% of homes. With the convergence of PC and TV equipment well advanced, barriers to receiving on-line services continue to recede. UK based retail sites vary from independent operators such as Lossie Seafoods to The Body Shop, Austin Reed and Toys R Us. There are also an increasing number of virtual shopping centres including Barclays'

BarclaySquare, the London Mall and Highland Trail which offers net access to Scottish products. Compuserve has opened its only customised non-US merchant service in the form of the UK Shopping Centre. Tenants include WH Smith, Dixons, Tesco and Virgin. Hard data about the relative success of these schemes is difficult to come by, but early figures are not particularly encouraging. Although estimates suggest that the BarclaySquare site received more than 200,000 visitors between its opening in May 1995 and March 1996, the Finance Director of Argos revealed that, after nine months on-line, the Argos web site had sold just 22 items.

Most retailers regard their web sites as experiments from which they will learn. A spokesperson for Dixons was entirely pragmatic: "By the end of the century I would be surprised if the home sector (including all electronic channels to market) was delivering for us the equivalent in sales of one average store. That would mean sales of up to £3 million, so it would be worth our while doing it, depending on the cost. But it will not have much impact on our high street operations."

Charles believes that when considering the potential for retailing on the Internet, it is important to remember that the Internet may not be perceived as the only, or indeed the most attractive, choice of electronic delivery channel by retailers. Case studies in France, the Netherlands and Germany in the report suggest that there are considerable debates over the technical obstacles to widespread Internet usage in these countries. Current investments by retailers such as Quelle and Ahold in Germany and the Netherlands and La Redoute in France are devoted as much to CD-ROM and CDi as to Internet routes to market, whereas the UK has been less involved with CD-ROM development. Retailers actively involved in electronic channels comment that, despite longer term trends towards technical convergence, the different systems and standards presently available make parallel developments prohibitively expensive.

A truly profitable, transactional presence on the Internet is rather more problematic than many of its proponents would have retailers believe. European retailers may not find this conclusion in itself surprising, but they should not find in it grounds for complacency. The choice of consumers in the market place will be extended with or without the assistance of traditional retail organisations. The success of electronic channels to market is not likely to be determined solely by retail presence or absence and the challenge of profitable operation whilst a complex one, may not be avoidable in a future business environment.

The research on which Charles' article is based was carried out by the Oxford Institute of Retail Management on behalf of KPMG. It forms part of a series of studies into the strategic uses of technology and its impact on European retailers. The research includes a series of frameworks against which a retailer's positioning strategy can be judged as well as an analysis of the widely different experience of Internet usage in a number of European countries.[12]

Many of the problems encountered by retailers entering the online shopping market are those experienced in the past by mail order and home shopping companies. In one of their *Market Direction* reports, Euromonitor have looked at the mail order industry in France, Italy, Germany, Spain, the United States and the United Kingdom.[13] The future outlook for mail order indicates steady progress rather than spectacular growth. Mail order houses are anticipated to continue gaining share at the expense of department stores. The report identifies areas of the mail order trade where most competition can be anticipated. For example, mail order faces stiffer competition from category killers and DIY sheds in the important home furnishings market.

The fashion retailer Burton has predicted an explosion of electronic shopping when mass access becomes possible through television in a few years' time. The Debenhams, Top Shop and Dorothy Perkins group has added web sites for its Hawkshead and Racing Green brands through which customers can buy products. Burton has bombarded consumers with 2.6 million mail order catalogues over recent months in an effort to build its home shopping arm. Chief executive John Hoerner said "At present the knowledge of how to access the net is the hardest part. In three years' you will be able to get on through the television. It will be as easy as using a VCR and that will expand the market from five million to 22 million." He said business on the Internet was minimal at present, with the number of transactions completed only in the low hundreds. "At the moment it's all about the sex appeal and very little about business. It's not remotely close to being meaningful. But the ultimate future is it will be a great way to sell things." Burton now has transactional Internet sites for all its main brands, and has upgraded the existing site for the 'Innovations' catalogue acquired a year ago.

In the *International Retail Banking Yearbook* there is a section which considers the impact of technology on retail banking.[14] In particular, Lafferty reports on the new age of 'cyberbanking' in the US. Here the growth in numbers of modems in American households has provided US retail banks with a ready-made infrastructure for a new wave in home banking. After a decade of false starts and failed experiments, PC-driven home banking is finally taking off in the US. Remote banking is already available to most who want it in the US, with one-quarter of US banks offering the service by telephone – either touch-tone or person-to-person – to 75-80% of retail users. The *Yearbook* also reports on the progress of direct banking in the UK. Following the success of the Midland Bank's 'First Direct' operation the remaining retail banks are all now entering the market. Most of the new generation are add-on units, designed to remove the need to visit a branch for the majority of everyday services, rather than clones of Midland's unique branded operation. Most of the earliest services to be launched have targetted higher net worth individuals before spreading to a wider customer base. National Westminster's 'Primeline', which offered person-to-person contact to 20,000 account holders, is an example of one such service. The concept of selling financial services via the telephone was pioneered by the Royal Bank of Scotland's 'Direct Line'. 'Direct Line' has revolutionised the general insurance market in less than ten years and has now moved on to selling more complex life and investment products. It is in areas such as banking and insurance that the concept of online shopping has had most success.

Online bookselling is, without a doubt, the single most spectacular hit in general consumer retailing since the Internet business gold rush began, and the key competitor is a company no one had even heard of two years ago.[15] The US-based Amazon now describes itself as the world's largest bookstore, with some justification. Its finely-tuned computerised ordering system can find almost any title you want and despatch it to you within a matter of days, often at a discount of up to 40% off the price you find in the bookstores. The battle for UK book buyers is just beginning. Waterstones has now gone on the Web to compete with a number of existing networks including 'Bookpages', a lively site with much the feel of Amazon. The successful sale of books has encouraged Amazon to expand its operations into online retailing of over-the-counter drugs.

The importance of price – and ultimately margin – in sucessful online retailing is usually paramount. Online customers expect a deal in return for the work they put in to place an order and the expense of being on the Net. Without keen prices they will simply shop elsewhere. In terms of pure revenues, the most successful online site is Dell's direct PC service, where an interactive page allows users to design and "build" PCs to their own specification. This is currently bringing in business to the tune of around £1.8 million per working day through Dell's sites around the world, including the UK. Virtually every other PC and computer manufacturer of any size is now seeking to emulate Dell's success by creating similar sites. Such is the volume of sales through direct online orders that analysts expect the channel to have significant repercussions on other distribution methods in the next year.

The same pressures are becoming obvious in the area of finance. In the US, there has been a race in the broking community to provide Web-based share-trading services offering instant access to traders and commission fees far below those associated with conventional systems. In the UK, Eagle Star recently introduced a 15% discount for all car insurance policies taken out on its new site. According to US analysts, one key area set to emerge as a Net winner in Europe over the next year is travel. Thomas Cook has started a lively UK site, but at the moment it lacks the ability to check availability on flights while you are online, something which US sites – and their customers – now tend to take for granted.

One area which is increasingly attracting interest is that of online small ads. *Auto Trader*, the used-car magazine, recently unveiled its new Web site listing around 100,000 secondhand vehicles. Could online small ads be big business? Microsoft certainly thinks so. It has started a number of city guides in the US under the 'Sidewalk' banner that are just the sort of mix of listings and ads found in conventional magazines. Bill Gates isn't well known for chasing losers. If 'Sidewalk' prospers, it will probably be proof that yet another form of conventional business is open to competition from new digital media on the Web.

According to *Interact*, the newsletter of the Interactive Media in Retail Group, there are three main lessons to be learnt in the area of online retailing.[16] The first lesson is that the growth is there. Even in these early days, the market shows consistent growth in line with projections that indicate a global market worth $1,000 million in 1997, which will more than double every year to nearly $7,000 million by 2000. Certain sectors will dominate the market. Computer products will comprise one of the largest segments, as hardware sales increasingly move to electronic channels. Software distributors, led by initiatives from Microsoft will begin to deliver products online. Travel and entertainment will be significant markets, as online channels make inroads into the volume business currently carried by a combination of telephone, teletext services and printed classifieds.

Second, online demographics are beginning to be better understood. Other than computers and travel, successful online merchants tend to be in the classic mail-order businesses such as books, music CDs, videos, men's casualwear, flowers, technology products and gift items. More women consumers will not change this mix in the short term. The distribution operations of many products that appeal to women – cosmetics, clothes, personal care products – will be uneconomic and one of the biggest potential areas – groceries – relies on complex staffing and premises requirements. Third, the 'Protected by SET' logo appearing on commercial sites, demonstrating adoption of the Microsoft, Netscape, Visa and MasterCard 'Secure Electronics Transaction' standard, will go a long way to dispelling any remaining fears about security of credit card payments online.

The retail analyst Verdict has produced projections in all areas of retailing to the year 2001.[17] For example, the growth in sales for department stores, non-specialist stores and second-hand goods retailers. Verdict also looks at growth rates for non-store retailers from 1987 through to the year 2001. This includes home shopping and mail order. A general outlook is provided, summarising forecasts for all retailers sales 1987-2001. Mintel has produced a *Special Report* along similar lines looking in detail at the market for home shopping, including mail order, direct selling and direct response.[18]

According to Verdict the mail order market grew by 3.4% in 1996, reversing the decline of the previous year when sales fell by 2.1%.[19] This turnaround was due to the steady growth in direct mail order which accounted for 20.1% of the total market, up from 18.5% in 1995. Direct mail order benefited from the rising proportion that it accounts for of the sales of the big 5 agency companies. Agency sales continued their inexorable decline in real terms.

Home shopping is seen as an immensely broad sector, encompassing virtually all non-food product areas. Although catalogues remain the most popular selling format, the market also includes direct selling, party plans and, more recently, electronic shopping via television or the Internet. The market is dominated by the agency companies who, like direct mail order businesses, use catalogues to sell a wide range of products. However, agency companies offer free credit with easy repayment terms, a USP which is targeted at lower income groups. Direct catalogues only offer interest bearing credit and, without the cost of financing interest free credit, are able to pitch prices below the agency titles.

Despite this diversity this is probably the most highly concentrated form of retailing, with a handful of companies dominating the sector. The 'big five' agency operators – GUS, Littlewoods, Freemans, Grattan and Empire – account for the vast majority of home shopping sales. Verdict calculate that these companies accounted for 59.7% or £4,507 million of all home shopping sales in 1996.

Despite the increasing demand for more convenient methods of shopping, home shopping sales are declining. Mail order and direct selling enable people to shop in the comfort of their own homes without the time and expense involved in high street shopping. There is a growing market of consumers who are 'cash rich but time poor' for whom mail order should be an attractive proposition. Yet these higher spenders are the least likely to use catalogues or other home shopping methods. The home shopping market may have improved, offering customers a wider range of products and better service, but it has inherent disadvantages which puts it in a weak position when it comes to competing with high street retailers. Home shopping may be a convenient method of ordering goods but it has major drawbacks when it comes to selecting and receiving products. For many consumers the pleasure of shopping comes from visiting stores which can offer 'real' convenience, offering personal service, a wide range of products and instant availability.

According to Verdict the home shopping market was worth £7,551 million in 1996. The 3.4% sales increase represents a significant improvement on the 2.1% decline in 1995, but home shopping still underperformed the pace of growth of all retail sales. The result is that home shopping accounts for 4.5% of all retail sales – its lowest level over the past ten years.

The inexorable decline of the agency market is continuing. The trend to targeted direct mail order catalogues was accelerated by some agency companies themselves, with Littlewoods' 'Index Extra' and Empire's 'La Redoute' & 'Vertbaudet' books all being expanded fast. Verdict argues that the success of these and other direct titles will be crucial to the growth of these companies in the light of the continuing decline in agency business. Pressures on traditional agency mail order will intensify as more high street retailers move into home shopping. Marks & Spencer is to launch a fashion catalogue early next year, making its exclusive brand available more widely, especially to areas only served by a small M&S store. The Burton Group's acquisition of 'Racing Green' and 'Innovations' heralds the development of a home shopping operation which will provide additional channels of distribution for its fashion brands.

Home shopping is the most international area of retailing. New entrants such as Eddie Bauer from America are launching catalogues and the market will face increasing competition from foreign companies. Electronic home shopping, including TV shopping channels and the Internet, grew its share of the market but still accounts for only 1% of home shopping or 0.04% of retail sales. The report argues that there is neither the technology nor the demand from the public at present to stimulate growth. Grocery superstores continue to develop various home shopping tests. However, developments are still in their early stages as companies struggle to make delivering profitable and overcome the problems of fulfilment. The big agency companies all increased the amount of branded merchandise within their catalogues. This mirrors the trend in the high street and is leading to the establishment of points of competitive differentiation in a sector notorious for its sameness. There was a marked difference in performance between the big five agency companies, with the smaller players, together with Littlewoods, increasing market share. Grattan and Empire achieved the largest rises relative to their size. In part this was due to growth in their direct businesses, but they also managed to increase their agency sales (Table 4.2).

Table 4.2 Home Shopping Market Shares 1996

GUS	24.2%
Littlewoods	16.1%
Grattan	7.7%
Freemans	7.4%
Empire	4.5%
N Brown	4.2%
Fine Art	3.1%
Next	3.1%
Direct selling	13.2%
Other	16.4%

Despite having had a difficult year, GUS is moving from being systems-led to being more market-driven. GUS has the resources and management expertise to develop its direct business and Verdict believes that the appointment of Lord David Wolfson as Chairman heralds a major period of retail-led change. The future of Littlewoods will be linked to that of Freemans, which has been put up for sale by Sears. This takeover is expected to be approved by the Monopolies and Mergers Commission (MMC) and will lead to a much larger group able to challenge GUS for market leadership. With greater dynamism evident from Littlewoods Home Shopping management, this challenge will be a determined one. Verdict conclude their report with a useful analysis of high street retailing versus home shopping.

In an FT report that appeared in 1997 Ian Thompson agrees with Verdict's view that the home shopping sector, traditionally characterised by agency 'shopping clubs' and direct catalogue companies, is undergoing enormous change.[20] Emerging new channels are enabling businesses to sell direct to consumers using the telephone, CD-ROM, interactive TV, online services and the Internet, without the prohibitive startup costs and overheads associated with conventional and mail-order retailing. The world's largest retail groups are taking a fresh look at home shopping, and many of them are acquiring or setting up direct selling schemes aimed at defending market shares in this highly competitive arena. An increasing array of products – from financial and travel services to clothing, gadgets and groceries – can now be ordered via these new channels and delivered direct to the home.

Over the next few years, emerging channels look set to alter the shape of the home shopping landscape, as well as redefine the role of the retailer. One result of this change already apparent is the increase in takeover activity in the store and catalogue shopping sectors, as Sears, GUS, Marks and Spencer, Tesco and other major players consolidate by acquiring or setting up new direct sales channels alongside their traditional operations. Meanwhile, new entrants are coming into the market, building a customer base and threatening many of the established retailers.

The success of home shopping channels in many sectors – grocery retailing, computer hardware and software, travel products, music and books – suggests that a new marketing paradigm is emerging. Contemporary marketing theory now stresses the emergence of a new market in which the customer is more enlightened, more informed and has greater choice. Shopping is increasingly regarded as a time-wasting chore, and middlemen are being cut out of loops everywhere as customers go direct to suppliers. Conventional sales processes are becoming derailed as suppliers increasingly find themselves taking part in a succession of beauty parades, where price, standards of customer service and after-care are the criteria. Fragmentation of the market means that customer acquisition is paramount, and that means retailers must offer every aspect of the transaction chain – information gathering, advice, finance, fulfilment, after-care – at multiple points of sale, running in parallel on each channel.

Thompson's report tracks the best estimates of realistic growth patterns, current demography and commercial activity, using authoritative surveys and sources to provide an up-to-date, accurate snapshot of the home shopping sector now, and its likely development and potential in the foreseeable future.

In an earlier report, Liz Mandeville confirms home shopping to be at the centre of intense discussion and speculation.[21] There is a widespread expectation that its share of the market will grow rapidly as a result of growing use of electronic networks for all forms of communication. There is also an opposite view, which points to the small share of retail expenditure devoted to home shopping as evidence that no swift or rapid increase is to be expected. The figure varies between 2% and 5% in different parts of Europe. If home shopping does take off, then it will offer opportunities for some and threats to others:

- traditional retailers will be faced particularly with the challenges of making use of shop space and managing home deliveries

- mail order companies have all the necessary facilities for taking and fulfilling orders, but have yet to demonstrate that they have the ability to grow the market above its existing modest size – mail order represents a flat as well as small percentage of total retail expenditure

- distribution companies have a good deal to gain from home shopping

- manufacturers will find different avenues for addressing the public, and those with leading brands will probably be able to sell at terms more advantageous to them than at present

- advertising agencies face particularly clear challenges, as online services pass the initiative to customers and the boundaries between fact and image come under scrutiny.

Overall, European industry will find home shopping a challenge, as the internationalisation which it allows will provide opportunities for foreign companies to penetrate this market. This applies both to retailers and to suppliers of the home shopping infrastructure. The market could move much more rapidly if the European Commission's information society vision is realised. The synergy of home shopping with other services to the home is a positive strength if the communications infrastructure is present, but it makes the future of home shopping dependent on these developments. Should the information society prove elusive, home shopping will be restricted in its growth. If the vision is realised, then online services of all kinds will become routine, and home shopping will take a quarter or more of the retail market by 2000. Mandeville believes the most likely outcome to be one where movement towards the information society is patchy, and issues of a legal, fiscal, commercial, and standards–related nature have to be settled before the market can grow strongly. There will almost certainly be significant growth in home shopping, but at a more modest level (Table 4.3).

Table 4.3 Prospects for home shopping in Europe in 2000

Food sales via home shopping	10-15%
Non-food sales via home shopping	20-25%
Main communications media	Cable, telephone (Internet)
Most popular home devices	(1) TV plus set-top box (2) PC-based communicating multi-media device
Largest market	Two-income professional households
Still growing	TV shopping
Falling	Catalogue mail order
Overall winners	Existing mail order companies (but under a different name) Packagers of online services to the home; Software houses Distribution companies Owners of infrastructure Manufacturers of leading brands Highly efficient large retail companies Small retail high street specialists with high service level; Youngish professionals
Overall losers	Retailers who opt out Less efficient retailers Traditional advertising agencies Retailers and banks with large property holdings Lesser brands Manufacturers of in-store equipment The old, frail, poor

(**Source**: author's research (Liz Mandeville) and estimates)

Home shopping is the latest scheme at Iceland, the frozen foods chain, which has been struggling to re-invent itself in the face of opposition from superstores armed with loyalty cards and extended opening hours.[22] Research shows that 65% of Iceland customers do not have access to a car during the day, so a home delivery service was started in September 1997. Reaction to the new service has been positive, not only increasing sales to existing customers – who only used to buy what they could carry – but also attracting new customers. Iceland now has a fleet of 900 vans and drivers for home delivery, which can reach 95% of the nation's households.

Iceland has run a home shopping trial for the past two years – first in 20 stores and then in 100 – and is now preparing to go nationwide with it. The snag is that only 6% of Iceland's customers are interested in home shopping and the group will have to capture shoppers from its bigger rivals. Iceland are pinning big hopes on its venture into home shopping – at present its stores make about £37,000 a week in sales, compared with £500,000 or so at a Tesco Metro (one of the small inner-city convenience stores).

As 1997 drew to a close, Europe's online cash registers appeared decidedly empty.[23] Indeed, while US companies such as Amazon.com were busy racking up sales, Europe spent a frustrating 1997 attempting to overcome daunting hurdles in the area of electronic commerce. Language and currency problems, tax and distribution hang-ups, and a lacklustre audience were among the dilemmas retailers faced. "What we've seen over this year was the influx of new ideas and new providers of e-commerce sites," says Chris Buerger, senior business analyst at market research group Datamonitor. "Next year we're hoping for the domino effect." Putting those new ideas into practice certainly hasn't been easy. Europe is home to more than 20 different languages and currencies. A consumer in Sweden might wish to buy chocolates from a famous Italian chocolatier, but find it impossible to read the directions on the Web site or calculate how much the truffles cost in his native kronor. Likewise, many retailers still rely on local or state-run courier services that can't guarantee timely cross-border delivery.

"We're a family-run business that would love to reach a bigger audience across Europe," says Fiona Hunter, public relations manager for Bettys & Taylors of Harrogate by Post, a small tea and cake business in Yorkshire, England. The small company felt daunted by the big online world until it recently got involved in a large pan-European e-commerce initiative sponsored by Microsoft. "Going about the language and delivery issues is an enormous, scary task," says Ms Hunter. Taxes, too, have been a problem. Many of Europe's governments, worried about losing revenue to cyberspace, have implemented haphazard tax policies that have hampered online shopping. Take CD sales in the Netherlands: small foreign firms operating over the Internet currently offer compact disks at cheaper rates than Dutch stores and mail them without customs declarations so that the consumer isn't charged Europe's hefty value-added tax. To get around the problem, a year ago the Dutch government ordered the post office to open all packages that looked like they might contain a CD, adding two weeks to delivery time and extra charges for consumers.

In some places, the Internet simply can't keep up with the competition. In the early 1980s, many European countries came up with proprietary online systems and encouraged the public to get online. These systems are still thriving. In France, 30% of homes use Minitel, a network set up by France Telecom that now has over 17 million users. And in Germany, Deutsche Telekom runs a service called T-Online that has nearly two million active subscribers.

Perhaps one of the biggest problems, however, is that Europe is still woefully offline. Market research firm Inteco Corp. estimates that only 19% of European homes have PCs, compared with about 38% in the US. Worse, market researchers estimate 90% of European homes have yet to access the Internet, largely because telephone rates are still so high in Europe as to make surfing a luxury.

"All these issues – so many of them – have combined to keep e-commerce tucked away in the 'too difficult' file for a long time," says Jame Roper, managing director of Interactive Media in Retail Group, a trade association. "But we had to start somewhere."

Indeed, with so many hurdles, it was inevitable that European pioneers in the field would run up against some disappointments. One of the most notorious early examples was popular UK retailer Argos Plc, a company with total sales of £1.66 billion last year. Argos burst onto the online scene with a fanfare, putting a number of its most popular items online and situating itself in a much-trumpeted UK cybermall. But according to retail analysts, the company managed to sell just 22 items in its first nine months on the Internet market. Argos won't confirm those numbers, but it does admit that its Internet sales in 1996 fell short of £2,000.

The UK was also the home of another first in the online shopping world in 1997. Tesco Plc attempted an online food shopping trial. But the limitations of the experiment were soon evident. Because the goods must be delivered fresh, only surfers in certain postal codes could participate. Those that did needed to order a CD-ROM that could take several weeks to be delivered through the normal mail. And shoppers had to schedule times to wait at home for groceries to be delivered. Tesco wouldn't disclose user numbers, though it says it is reaching its targets. Analysts, however, aren't so sure. "The beauty of online shopping is that it makes things easier," says Petra Gartsen, an analyst at Dataquest, the market research unit of US-based Gartner Group. "But early online grocery shopping tests have just proven to be a hassle."

These days, European retailers are getting smarter, attempting to build on already proven strategies. Hoping to capitalize on the German love for mail-order catalogues, for example, large German mail-order companies Quelle Schickendanz AG and Otto Versand GmbH have both recently migrated their selling strategies to the Web. Another German mall, called 'My World', a creation of giant retailer Karstadt AG, has wisely linked itself to Germany's proprietary T-Online service. The tactics seem to be working. Datamonitor estimates that two-thirds of all the online consumer sales in Europe take place in Germany.

Perhaps even more importantly, big business has stepped up to lend a helping hand. One of the most publicized was a project called 'SurfAndBuy', piloted by International Business Machines Corp. IBM decided to focus on France, and convinced some fifty well-known French retail firms to participate. IBM kept costs low and legal issues to a minimum – retailers had only to sign a single-page contract. IBM then worked with all the retailers to develop special online promotions that consumers might not find on Minitel. So far, statistics for the site have been encouraging. In the first month it had 70,000 visitors, and 2.3 million hits in total. At this point, the site is pulling in about 20-25,000 French francs a day.

Yet another daring adventure currently under way is spearheaded by a consortium including Microsoft, Hewlett-Packard, KPMG, United Parcel Service of America, Visa International and Europay International. Hoping to tackle those problems most daunting to pan-European online shopping, the group pooled its resources and came up with a project called 'e-Christmas'. More than 200 merchants across Europe got involved. UPS undertook the mammoth task of working out the total cost for delivery, taxes and tariffs for each gift on the site for 27 countries in the world. Visa and Europay International worked on a secure payment system, which showed prices in different currencies. The site, which ran from mid-November until Christmas 1997, was available in six different languages.

"There were so many issues we hadn't thought of that 'e-Christmas' managed to package together comprehensively," says Rebecca Whittingham-Boothe, marketing manager for Stanfords Map & Travel Bookshop, one of the participants. No one in the 'e-Christmas' group claimed participants would be much richer after the pilot. However, the project convinced many of Europe's retailers to face some fundamental problems and develop solutions.

As we have seen, there isn't a hotter subject in the computer industry today than the Internet. A search of Nexis, the newspaper database, shows thousands of articles containing the word 'Internet' every month. Wall Street loves the word, too – venture capital seems to pour into anything remotely Internet-related, and stocks of Internet-related companies are among the most actively traded. Amidst all this interest – or, as some would call it, hype – is a central paradox. The Internet is still far from mainstream. Despite all the hype, many retailers are still not familiar with what the Internet is, how it got started, or how it works.[24]

For retailers, the major question is whether the World Wide Web is now, or ever will be, an effective medium for selling. How they answer that question depends to some extent on which experts they choose to believe. Kurt Salmon Associates, for example, predicted in a report in 1995 that non-store retailing will account for 55% of total retail sales by 2010.

The dramatic rise, from the current 15% of sales, will be driven by consumer demand for customization and instant service, and enabled technologies such as Interactive TV and the Internet, the consulting firm said. The Web has an increasing number of success stories. Among them is Roswell Computer Books, Halifax, Nova Scotia, Canada. The proprietor, Roswell James, claims he more than doubled his sales by being on the Web, essentially transforming his remotely located single book store into a successful international business. Roswell Books is part of the Nova Scotia Technical Network mall, one of hundreds of so-called "cybermalls" that have sprouted up on the Web. Links to many of them can be found through a Web site called 'The Hall of Malls'. Cybermalls on the Web are large and small, broad and specialized. They are also international – a cybermall in London or Singapore can be reached from an American users' computer just as quickly and seamlessly as a cybermall in New York. Most cybermalls are created by local service providers with enough marketing and technical know-how to get relatively small retailers up and selling on the Net. Some of the large players getting into the cybermall business include MCI (http://www.internetmci.com), the Internet Shopping Network (http://www.internet.net), Surfin' UTC (http://www.shoputc.com), Cybershop (http://www.homeshop.com), Virtual Vineyards (http://www.virtualvin.com), and Retail Info Center (http://www.retail-info.com).

What does the future hold for electronic commerce on the Internet? In the next few years we can expect a proliferation of companies offering "intelligent agents" to help consumers do their shopping. That's the view of Anderson Consulting, which recently launched an experimental intelligent agent, called 'Bargain-Finder', that allows users to compare prices for specific titles of, for example, compact discs among eight web sites that sell them.

It has long been recognised that the holy grail of the World Wide Web is e-commerce – doing business over the web.[25] But while companies in the computer field like Dell long ago realised their web site was a cool way of reaching potential customers, more traditional manufacturers, retailers and providers of financial services have trodden warily down the e-commerce route. In many ways, e-commerce for consumers is part of a continuum which dates back to the last century and catalogue/mail order shopping. Some of the greatest fortunes of the 20th century, including that of the Wolfson family in Britain, have been built on mail order. The busy or rural customer found it easier to shop from a catalogue delivered to the home and offering easy credit terms, rather than travelling to the high street.

In recent times with the increasing number of families with single parents or two working parents – and less time – downmarket catalogue retailing has been replaced with the highly fashionable home shopping concept. The masters of the wired catalogue of the 21st century will have the possibility of making the same fortunes as Sears Roebuck, Littlewoods and Empire have in the past. This is clearly the nettle which Gap, the San Francisco based clothing group, is seeking to grasp. Gap, with its focus on 'preppie' American style from the chino pants and button down cotton shirts, was a fashion winner on the high streets of the US and the UK until imitators who saw their market share falling moved onto its patch. The decision by Gap to launch itself onto the World Wide Web is an attempt to stay ahead of the predators moving into its territory. It is counting on an overlap between its upper-income level young customers and Internet users. Statistically, it would appear to be on the right track.

A report produced in 1998 by the DTI, *Moving into the Information Age*, provides some impressive data. The proportion of population, not just with PCs but actually online, is surging. In the United States, the world's largest consumer of goods, some

21% of the population is online, with Britain in its wake with 10% followed by Japan, Germany and France – with the penetration much lower in the latter three countries. The critical mass of internet users has driven corporations worldwide to set up a presence on the Web. According to the DTI data Japanese companies have surged into the lead on this front with 45% of them now having a presence on the web. They are followed by US firms where 41% of companies have web sites and the UK where the numbers have reached 37%. This is not just some passing fad for commerce. Business has learnt over recent decades that information technology is a critical key to commercial success on any scale.

In the City of London the arrival of screen based markets is driving the old open outcry form of trading off the map as is currently being seen on the options and futures market, Liffe. Nearly all share transactions, whether they are conducted by big investors like the Prudential, or the small investors, are now done electronically. An increasing volume of small shareholders are checking their share prices online. Moreover, they have signed up with financial services companies who provide them with programmes which allow them to deal in shares electronically; e-commerce is making popular capitalism that much easier. In fact, the financial services companies, building on the experience seen in markets, are among the first to see the opportunity of the internet. They have responded to a public demand for facilities where consumers can pay their bills, select their insurance products and carry out banking transactions in their own homes.

Several technologies are currently vying for supremacy. Direct selling down the telephone has been a winner with companies like Midland's 'First Direct' and the Royal Bank of Scotland's 'Direct Line', the first out the starting traps. Barclay's Bank recently launched a screen based financial service using telephones, a mid-point between telephone banking and PC banking. Lloyds TSB have been experimenting with video based home banking in Kingston-upon-Hull, in which the television zapper becomes the link to the bank.

Most of the banks, which are already offering software packages to small and medium-sized business to carry out their commercial transactions, will soon be doing the same for consumers. Nobody is certain, as yet, as to what the dominant financial services technology will be. But as more people are connected to the web and the cost of being connected falls, the PC – because of its enormous capacity and speed – offers perhaps an opportunity. There are, however, all kinds of resistances to be overcome before e-commerce becomes a serious challenger to the high street. Among the most difficult to overcome are complexity and cost. In purely practical terms a constraint on consumer e-commerce is security. Customers worldwide have been concerned that credit card and other banking data put onto the web, to make a purchase at the globe's largest bookshop Amazon or buy an insurance policy from the Norwich Union, will leave behind a footprint which even the novice hacker could decipher.

The UK government announced recently that it had dropped a mandatory licensing scheme, offering companies guaranteed safe trading on the Internet, and had decided to go with the voluntary scheme instead. This would promote measures like "electronic signatures" to authenticate electronic trading documents. It was decided to abandon the more formal approach after it found that many companies saw compulsory encryption as difficult to operate. Until the corporate sector can be assured that electronic contracts are valid and the consumer that their finances will not be plundered, this will be a naturally limiting factor for e-commerce.

Other problems for e-commerce include pricing strategies and social impact. In terms of pricing a company like Gap, with prices set differently in the US and Britain will have to decide if they are willing to give up margin – higher prices – for success on the web. But perhaps the most overwhelming difficulty of all for the web is that it is not democratic. The cost inhibiting factor from telephone lines to subscriptions to Internet providers means that it is only easily available to the better off A and B income groups with a smattering below. That may be great commercially, but will increase the divide between the 'have' and 'have–nots' in society. The Ford Model-T has yet to be discovered. Until telecoms and communications regulators and providers can devise a means of providing universal service at a lower price, e-commerce will be a divisive technology (Table 4.4).

A recent NOP survey has shown that British shoppers are finally catching on to the possibilities of the Internet. More than 10 million people in Britain now use the net, more than double the people logging on last year.[26] Companies are also beginning to realise the rich potential of net customers: the survey, done for Yahoo!, Ziff-Davis and KPMG, reveals that 70% of net users own their home or have a mortgage, and nearly half earn more than £25,000 a year. And 2 million Britons have used the web just to look around, before going on to buy the product online or at the nearest shop.

Table 4.4 Online Shopping – Forecast revenues from online shopping in the US, $million

	1999	2000
Computer products	1,228	2,105
Travel	961	1,579
Entertainment	733	1,250
Clothes	234	322
Gifts and flowers	386	658
Food and drink	227	336
Other	221	329
Total	**3,990**	**6,579**

(**Source**: Forrester Research Inc.)

Following the announcement in May 1998 by Gap that they will begin Internet selling, Toys 'R' Us and Autotrader have both revealed plans to introduce or expand sales over the Internet during the year. At the same time as Gap, Dial-a-cab, based in North London, launched its Internet cab-booking service – the first such service in the world. "Business over the Internet is certainly picking up," said a Toys 'R' Us spokesman, whose site at present contains a very limited number of products. "It's not a torrent, but we're starting to get lots of hits on the site and we will be expanding it over the next year." Both Tesco and Sainsbury's, whose Internet shopping services are so far limited to selected stores only, claim to have had extremely good reactions to online shopping. Both plan big expansions of their sites, which can also be reached by telephone or fax.

Of the supermarket giants Asda was the last to hold out against the home shopping revolution: its previous attempt to introduce it in a slightly different format in 1990 having flopped. Asda now plans to launch a grocery delivery service and online sales of home entertainment.[27] It also intends to try selling non-food products by satellite television as a first step towards running its own digital television home shopping channel. Asda sees such ventures as its preferred way forward, rather than seeking for a merger as a way of countering intense competition in a mature market with softening consumer demand. Analysts believe that while this strategy would work for the next five years there was concern about long term growth. In the past two years the group has held talks with both Safeway and Kingfisher and has looked at buying high street stores from Littlewoods and motorway service stations. Each time it has walked away. Asda's home delivery service will be based in south London and backed by a call centre, enabling Asda to target around 450,000 households within a six-mile radius. Customers will be able to order groceries through a catalogue containing 5,000 lines, delivered free to their homes. The Chief Executive Allan Leighton said the break-even for home delivery would be 500 orders per day at an average of £80 each. The warehouse would be built to handle around 1,000 orders daily. Online home shopping services were available by October 1998, initially in stores and through call centres. Leighton hopes to take this service on to the Internet, incorporating home entertainment and grocery shopping. All this will be a precursor to an Asda digital TV channel. The first taste of this will come when this year's Christmas range is launched through a series of six-minute satellite TV programmes.

Security is still one of the biggest worries for shops and shoppers, as research by Colin Germain at City University shows. Customers worry that hackers will get hold of their credit card details, and many find the idea of buying from an entirely faceless entity unnerving. Their worries may not be entirely theoretical: Germain concluded that only 55% of companies had a formal security policy, and nearly all were far from adequate. But as a spokesman for Tesco pointed out: "It's actually much easier to listen in to someone booking a theatre ticket over the telephone with their credit card" than to hack into most electronic commerce centres. Sixty-two per cent of the companies that took part in Germain's survey thought malicious action from employees was their major concern. "Ultimately, in the case of all credit card transactions, the customer has to trust the merchant's personnel not to illegally use their sensitive information," says Germain.

Bill McQuain is a busy marketing manager with Microsoft and his idea of quality time doesn't involve pushing a trolley round a supermarket. For the last few months he hasn't had to – McQuain has been using Tesco's Web site to order his weekly groceries, and each week a Tesco van delivers his shopping during a prearranged two-hour 'window'. "It's a marvellous service," he says, "I couldn't live without it."[28] Tesco was the first major supermarket chain to set up a transactional site, and its experience suggests that there is a large untapped market waiting for the first company to get its act together. Software house Interactive Developments, which designed the Tesco site, claims there has been an explosion in demand as retailers have become aware of the potential. They have also worked with Dixons to develop the first site retailing electrical goods, offering the surfer a range of 800 products to choose from. James Roper, of retail IT specialists IMRG, believes the traditional model for retail distribution is gradually being re-defined and that leading players will be established who will dominate the sector in the years to come. IMRG research suggests that online UK sales could reach £10 billion by 2001.

Tesco's first trial, based on the Osterley store in West London, started in February 1997. The trial was soon extended to four other stores, three in London and one in Leeds, and a sixth store, in Sutton, went online in July 1997. The site is functional and uncomplicated. Customers can choose from the full range of Tesco products and set delivery times and dates. Previous orders can be accessed and a running list kept offline and down-loaded to the store once the week's needs are known. Orders can be sent online or by phone or by fax. Tesco say that customer reaction has been "very exciting". Other sources say the company has been overwhelmed with demand for the service, with e-mails from all over the UK requesting that the pilot be extended nationwide. And the customers have come from new markets. Many, like McQuaid, are "time poor and cash rich", happy to pay the £5 delivery fee to escape from a Saturday afternoon chained to the trolley. But so far, Tesco says it has no immediate plans to go nationwide, due to a problem many other online suppliers have come across – order fulfilment.

Darryl Mattock's 'Internet Bookshop' has so far launched three times. With nearly a million titles on its database and detailed information about each title, the site generated interest immediately. But problems with meeting orders, and inadequate customer support, convinced Mattock that a much more sophisticated – and expensive – operation was essential. The inefficient ad hoc distribution arrangement with publishers and warehouses was scrapped and all orders are now fulfilled in house. Investment from the Blackwell family and a stock flotation provided the funds, and the site now enjoys deserved success, with 19% growth month on month and 15,000 new visitors each week.

Tesco's reluctance to go nationwide too soon stems from a desire to avoid the same problems. Currently, customer goods are "picked" by staff from the shelves of their local store and delivered in the company's vans. But consumers have experienced problems with orders sent to the wrong address and mistakes with quantities and similarly named items. Retail consultant Sally McNamee used Tesco's service regularly from its inception. "We were very excited to be involved and happy to pay the premium," she says. But so far, there has only been one fault-free delivery and Sally stopped using the service after a family weekend was ruined by a crucial order getting lost in the system. Sally would be willing to give the service another trial, but she feels that Tesco will have to look hard at its system.

Until recently, the retail presence on the Net has been focused on marketing. Like other businesses, retailers saw the Net as another advertising hoarding. But the advent of secure credit card transactions has radically changed the scene. SET (Secure Electronic Transaction) protocols allow credit card details to be encrypted and passed directly to the financial institution. The code could in theory be broken, but in practice the system is infinitely more secure than phone ordering. When the casual way most people pass their credit cards to any shop assistant is taken into account, online ordering is probably more secure.

However, retailers' interest is not explained just by the technical developments. In many ways the Net is coming of age. People have been online long enough to feel comfortable with the technology. Online demographics have also changed. The typical user is not the 19-year-old socially challenged 'anorak' depicted by the popular press. Instead we have the 35-year-old married professional with a young family. This AB group represents precisely the kind of market segment that companies would sell their grandmothers to get hold of. The result has been the rapid expansion of Net trading and a scramble to get on board the bus while there is still room. But it can be a bumpy ride. Roper makes the point: "Setting up the front end is relatively easy. The devil is in the detail." IBM's 'World Avenue' was launched in August 1996 with much fanfare, but apparently drew too little traffic for the 16 companies that had rented out virtual store-fronts in the mall. It closed a year after opening. The mall format has been adopted by a number of companies, including Barclays with 'BarclaySquare'. Commentators like sociologist Laurie Taylor argued that shoppers would be looking for a "real life" shopping experience. Actual experience suggests that shopping sites need to be focused and functional. Users want to log on, order the goodies and move on to something more interesting. The reason they are using the Net is because they don't like shopping. Replicating the shopping experience is unlikely to impress these consumers. What does seem to work on the Internet is niche trading. Cotton Oxford is the UK's largest retailer of rugby shirts. Its site went online in January 1997 aimed at the rugby connoisseur, with Lions tour updates and an ordering system based around a locker room and a kitbag. Cotton Oxford have generated some healthy business on the site, including sales from New Zealand and Norway – markets that the company hasn't had the resources to approach before. The most frequently quoted success story on the Net is that of Jack Scaife, a butcher from West Yorkshire, who sells traditional products like black pudding and ox tongue from a site that ships three tonnes of food a week worldwide. Scaife spotted the potential of the WWW for retailing at an early stage and is now reaping the rewards. It is a question of when, rather than if, the rest of the retail world will follow.

References

1   Reynolds J, Opportunities for Electronic Commerce, *European Retail Digest*, Issue 18, June 1998, p.5-9.

2   Datamonitor, *Online Digital Payments: 1997-2002* – London, 1998.

3   Market Assessment Publications, *Electronic Financial Commerce* – London, 1995.

4   Essinger J, *Virtual Financial Services* – London: FT Financial Publishing, 1996.

5   Fletcher A, EDI – *Electronic Commerce and the Internet* – Sutton: Reed Business Information, 1997.

6   Bourne S, The Future of Commerce on the Internet, *InfoNation Magazine*, 1997.

7   Thompson I, *The Infrastructure of Electronic Commerce: Building the New Digital Marketplace* – London: FT Media & Telecoms, 1997.

8   Caines R (ed.), *Home Shopping* – Hampton, Key Note, 1997.

9   Computer firms have hyped the future benefits of the Internet, *Shopping Centre*, February 1998, p2.

10 Field Christopher, *Retailing on the Internet: the Future for On-line Commerce* – London: FT Retail & Consumer Publishing, 1996.

11 Charles S, Retailing on the Internet, *Retail World*, Autumn 1996, p.11-12.

12 *The Internet: its Potential and Use by European Retailers* – London: KPMG Retail and Consumer Products Practice, 1996.

13 Euromonitor, *Mail Order and Home Shopping* (Market Direction) – London, 1994.

14 *International Retail Banking Yearbook* – Dublin: Lafferty Publications, 1995.

15 'Retail therapy on screen', *Sunday Times*, 2/11/97.

16 The Advance of Online Retailing, *Interact: the newsletter of the Interactive Media Retail Group*, Summer 1996.

17 Verdict, *Retailing 2001* – London, 1997.

18 Mintel, *Electronic Shopping* – London, 1996.

19 Verdict, *Home Shopping* – London, 1997.

20 Thompson Ian, *Home Shopping: the Revolution in Direct Sales* – London: FT Media & Telecoms, 1997.

21 Mandeville Liz, *Prospects for Home Shopping in Europe: Threats and Opportunities* – London: Pearson Professional, 1995.

22 Iceland's home shopping turns heat on rivals, *Guardian*, 25/3/98.

23 Europe's stores struggle to succeed online, *Wall Street Journal Europe*, 19/12/97.

24 Retailing on the Internet: seeking truth, beyond the hype, *Chain Store Age*, September 1995, p33-72.

25 Dash for cash in the online market place, *Guardian*, 27/5/98.

26 Net Gains, *Guardian*, 28/5/98.

27 Asda plans home shopping by digital television, *Guardian*, 26/6/98.

28 Off your trolley, *Guardian*, 3/7/97.

5. Conclusion: Shop 'Til You Drop

It is fair to say that in the UK today we are no longer a nation of shopkeepers but now a nation of shoppers. The traditional high street shop has been usurped by the explosion of the superstore. Consider the following selling points and it is impossible to conclude otherwise:-

- the number of UK supermarkets (defined as over 2,000 sq.ft. and with more than three checkouts) rose from 10 in 1949 to 4,764 in 1997. Superstores (over 25,000 sq.ft.) rose from four in 1965 to 1,052 in 1996

- sixty per cent of alcohol drunk at home comes from a supermarket, worth £3.5 billion a year

- Tesco estimates that it sells enough petrol in a year to get to the sun and back six times (2.9 gallons out of every 10 are bought at supermarkets)

- Scots are the most frequent shoppers in Britain, buying groceries 27 times in an eight week period. Shoppers in London and the South were the least frequent food shoppers, visiting grocery stores only 19 times in the same period

- Sainsbury's, the first UK retailer to start a fully-fledged bank, has seen its banking business grow by £50 a second since its launch in Febraury 1997

- supermarkets account for 20% of sales in the booming health and beauty industry, currently worth £8.9 billion a year

- Sainsbury's largest single transaction was at its Middlesbrough store in December 1989, when a businessman spent £12,242.

However, the direction of retailing is set to change all over again. As Bill O'Neill commented when writing in *The Guardian*, within five years the neighbours who still drive to the superstore, queue for a visa or push past browsers to reach the latest best-selling book will look ludicrous. They will be the technologically deprived underclass who, today, regard DIY as character-building, and computers as something best left to the kids. When Bill Clinton announced that the Internet should be a duty-free zone geared towards international trade, from online shopping to merchant banking, it represented an almost unprecedented appeal to the world to recognise the medium's huge potential. Clinton does not suggest that the Internet should be exploited without controls or guidelines, or without what he calls a "framework for global electronic commerce." He wants public servants in government and private companies to hold back from imposing their own tariffs and bringing down their own barriers for the sake of the international good.

Clinton's speech could be interpreted as the words of someone who has logged on and seen the future – and had a pretty good time in the process. Already there is something to be said for a surf of the trading sites on offer. Visionary zeal aside, and anoraks off, there is the bread and butter of everyday life, available in a convenient and secure environment destined to be even more so. Where once even experienced surfers worried about transmitting their credit-card details over the Net, agreements are now in place to ensure such details are encrypted to a level of security which makes telephone transactions seem foolhardy.

In the UK, so successful has been Tesco's trial of online shopping that the chain recently opened its sixth store. Dixons has also announced that, for the first time in the UK, shoppers will be able to buy washing machines, kettles and televisions online. Shoppers need a computer with an Internet connection; then it is just a question of grabbing their virtual shopping basket. At Tesco, there's the store's "award-winning" case of wine for £60. For summer reading, go to Amazon, where 'The Wisdom of the Bones' is available at $18.20 in hardback, against a recommended £18.99 in the high street. The Australian High Commission now advises travellers to register for a temporary visa online rather than queue. And British Airways claims that its online site has all the best deals. There are plenty of instances to show online shopping isn't perfect yet, but then neither is the real thing.

At the *Retail Week* & British Retail Consortium Conference held in March 1998 a number of key themes arose:

* alternative forms of retailing media such as digital television, catalogues and the Internet are a reality and are likely to pose a growing threat to existing forms of retailing. Retailers should therefore develop growth strategies taking these new formats into account

* as saturation dawns in national markets, the need to become a pan-European, or a global retailer, will become an increasingly important element in retailers'

development strategies. Food retailers in particular are leading the British assault abroad. Tesco, for instance, will this year open more new square footage outside the UK than in it. Eastern Europe will be the focus of this development, with France now considered too expensive to achieve any meaningful market share

- a strong brand image is important as a means of maintaining a point of difference and providing a compelling reason for consumers to shop with you. Furthermore, a strong brand name can enable you to diversify into new markets. However, retailers and manufacturers should be aware of the problems with 'overstretching' their brand name

- the 'traditional' customer is changing, in terms of her family structure and working life. With a growing number of women working there is a tendancy for retail and leisure activities to converge, into 'retailtainment' and 'edutainment'. Retailers must provide 'good value for time' (Henley Centre). This has implications for product presentation, the retail environment and service levels

- retailing in the UK is becoming more focused on the town centre with the government exerting more stringent controls on car usage and out-of-town development

- the term 'part-time' staff is redundant, instead staff should be referred to as 'key timers' employed to cover very specific times. With food stores now open 24-hours, everyone is in effect a 'key time' worker

- there is a need for sales staff to be 'passionate', enabling them to sell a brand as opposed to just a product, which in many cases can be purchased elsewhere.

Online shopping is not expected to replace the traditional retail culture; it will, however, be a significant adjunct. For the first three decades of the 21st century, it will be a secondary source of income for several existing top retail groups, and a primary revenue source for smaller but successful niche companies. As Koranteng says, "the question remains as to whether existing conventional retail store giants can make the switch to digital stores. In the US, Sears Roebuck's plans to generate extra income by going online seem to have backfired, at least for the moment. Also, major international music retail chains such as Virgin Megastore and Tower Records hesitate about online commerce in case the latter takes away business from existing physical stores, into which they have invested several million dollars."[1] Whatever else happens, the retailers must be prepared to devote as much time to operating online stores as they would to conventional shops. There is a constant need to update prices and special offers, otherwise the potential customer loses faith and, in the vast Internet universe, need never come back.

The cult of the 'mega-mall' approached its zenith in September 1998 with the opening of the Trafford Centre, Peel Holdings' £600 million retail and leisure complex on Manchester's south-western fringe. As Groom and Jones reported, the Centre hopes for 30 million visitors a year from across north-west England, making it one of the biggest out-of-town centres in the UK. It was also among the last to be approved by the government before planning rules were tightened. The slightly smaller mall at Cribbs Causeway, near Bristol, opened earlier in 1998. Bluewater, similar in scale to Trafford, will open next spring near Dartford in north Kent, followed by Braehead, Scotland's first big out-of-town complex. This £1.5 billion investment wave brings Britain's network of regional out-of-town centres to eight. They will be in most areas of the country, leading some observers to conclude that when John Gummer, the former Conservative environment secretary changed the rules in 1996, it was a limited triumph for opponents of out-of-town shopping.

Although no new proposals have come forward, the battle of the malls − accused of taking trade from neighbouring towns and creating traffic pollution − may not be over yet. They are popular with shoppers − so much so that older centres want to expand. Some argue they should be redesignated as town centres in their own right, as office and leisure use grows, evading the planning curbs. North-west towns are nervous about the Trafford Centre's impact. A survey commissioned by the Association of Town Centre Managers, published in November 1997, indicated some towns would suffer big losses in trade before they picked up again. Altrincham and Stockport were predicted to lose 27% in the first three years and Warrington 24%, while smaller centres such as Bolton and Blackburn would lose 15%. Even Manchester city centre, seen as the strongest retail centre, was forecast to lose 5% before custom picked up again. Other surveys suggested an 11% loss. The study has led 27 towns to form a consortium to fight the threat.

Richard Doidge, head of retail research at analysts Colliers Erdman Lewis, said these towns must redefine their market. Those such as Stockport would have the hardest task "but, if the past is anything to go by, the cake will , in the long run, get bigger and spending in retail centres will continue to rise." Cribbs Causeway is attracting 230,000 shoppers a week, slightly above expectations. "People are coming from beyond Taunton, Cardiff, Worcester and Newbury," said Jonathan Duckworth, centre manager. He said trade in Bristol city centre was 8% down, less than some feared. Many believe the real trend is not out-of-town, but the tendancy of big centres, whether in-town or out, to take market share from smaller ones. This clouds the issue of designation. In 1997 an extension to accommodate a department store at Merry Hill, West Midlands, was rejected after a planning inquiry. The inspector said conditions had to be fulfilled before the centre, in the middle of a conurbation, could be considered a town in its own right, and thus escape out-of-town restrictions. Chelsfield, the developer, is now adding restaurants, a larger cinema and a second hotel, building bridges to nearby Brierley Hill high street, and supporting a light rail link with Birmingham. The issue will also be at the heart of a planning inquiry in February 1999 into a £50 million expansion of the Metro Centre on Tyneside. "We are more or less Gateshead's town centre," said Ron Woodman, marketing manager. Eight local councils objected, but Brian McGurk, retail director at DTZ Debenham Thorpe, said many, such as Newcastle, Sunderland and Durham, were successful despite the Metro Centre. Smaller towns such as Morpeth, Hexham and Consett had a problem, he said, but were losing custom to a variety of outlets. The Council for the Protection of Rural England, which campaigned for curbs on out-of-town shopping, is unimpressed by the argument that the new centres are really towns. "They are ersatz town centres," said Henry Oliver, planning officer. "They close at night and have security guards. They are not a public domain like the centre of a city."[2]

In September 1998 the Office of Fair Trading (OFT), which is supervised by the DTI, published a report suggesting that no new laws were required to address the extraordinary control the superstores exert over their suppliers. As the journalist George Monbiot comments, "despite driving farmers and manufacturers out of business by forcing them into restrictive contracts and then paying less than the price of production for their goods, British superstores still manage to charge 40% more to their customers than stores on the Continent, with the result that they make three times as much money. As control over their suppliers was to have been the main inquiry into superstores' profits, it looks as if they will yet again be let off the hook."[3] Two earlier 'investigations' by the OFT and the Monopolies and Mergers Commission concluded that the superstores' market dominance, predatory pricing and uncompetitive practices, while wiping out small shops, posed no threat either to healthy competition or to the wider public interest.

When John Gummer announced that there would be no more out-of-town superstores, it looked as if their power would be curbed. In truth, the ruling has achieved precisely the opposite, which was surely why it was allowed to happen.

While Tesco, Sainsbury's and the others had already lined up enough planning consents to keep expanding for years to come, the door was conveniently slammed shut on the continental warehouses trying to enter the market. Even so, the British superstores are shrugging off these restrictions as blithely as they have disposed of all the others. Now, as Tesco links up with Esso, and Safeway develops its relationship with BP, the superstores have discovered in the petrol stations a new and largely unregulated frontier of out-of-town development. Monbiot believes the "end-game is already being played. Having crippled village shops, Sainsbury's is allowing them to stock its own products. Having helped create 'food desserts' in Britain's poorest places, Tesco has the government's blessing to move back into them, on its own terms." Whilst Tesco may be claiming to create a further 10,000 jobs over the next year, it has been shown that the growth of superstores does in fact destroy jobs. A National Retail Planning Forum report shows that a new superstore costs, on average, a net 276 local jobs, as independent grocers, village shops, newsagents and milk rounds close down. The out-of-town superstore "creates neither choice nor convenience, but merely concentrates them, laying waste to the diversity of social and economic life outside the store, shattering community, cluttering our streets with traffic."

As has been shown thoughout this guide to the literature, the retail industry impacts upon all our lives. The growth in out-of-town retailing has laid waste the traditional high street whilst at the same time creating a leisure phenomenon all of its own. What will the future hold for retailing? Whilst recent years have seen a move towards the pre-eminence of the out-of-town superstore it seems that this has plateaued and there may be a long-overdue resurgence in the fortunes of the high street. Town centres have started to resist the apparent dominance of the large out-of-town retailers. Cardiff city centre, for example, has run a television campaign against out-of-town shopping. The city's decision to fight back against out-of-town shopping follows the research published in September 1998 by the Department of Environment showing that superstores have cut the market share of food retailers in market towns by 50%. In a recent national survey, Cardiff was voted top for shops in the UK – above London's West End, Manchester, Bristol, Birmingham and Edinburgh. But factory villages to the north and west, rejuvenated shopping centres in valley towns and Newport, and The Mall at Cribbs Causeway, near Bristol, have started to compete. The Mall boasts a £750,000 advertising budget and 6.3 million visitors in the first six months since opening in March 1998. Jonathan Duckworth, manager at The Mall, says customers are attracted by easy access and parking and the convenience of 130 shops and restaurants under one roof. It is complementary to, not in direct competition with, town and city centres, he insists. Back in Cardiff, though, store managers see a threat and the retail partnership was set up to coordinate the fight back.[4]

In the last year or so it seems that retailers' interest in the high street has been revived. This is, in part, due to the tighter restrictions in place under which retailers must now prove there is no suitable site in, or near, the town centre before being granted out-of-town planning permission. But it is also because retailers and local authorities are working more closely together to improve high streets in the large cities and towns. The local threat of Cribbs Causeway has, for instance, forced Bristol's local authority to team up with retailers to protect the central shopping district from the effects of such a vast out-of-town development. "Authorities are really getting their act together on the high street," says Ms Jane Blower, property affairs manager of Sainsbury's. "They are trying to make town centres more accessible and there is a greater blend of facilities than there used to be."[5] This has caused retailers to rethink their approach to the high street shopper. Instead of an all-purpose service, increasingly consumers want to wander down the high street, either to compare goods on offer, such as clothing or cameras, or to top up their main weekly shop. Witness Tesco's Metro concept, a smaller supermarket aimed at the working man or woman who wants to buy portable items such as fresh vegetables or ready meals; or Mothercare, which is shifting its bulky goods such as prams and cots to out-of-town sites but investing in its fashion offer in the high street. "It is a matter of understanding that the customer shops in lots of different places at different times," says Mr Bernard Hughes of Tesco.

As a result, the high street is beginning to reclaim a greater proportion of planned development. Some 1.3 million sq. metres of shopping centre space is scheduled to be built in town centres by the turn of the century, as against 687,800 sq. metres out-of-town. But retailers are also choosy about where they are prepared to locate in the town centre. While the high street does not appear to be short of potential residents, secondary streets remain unattractive to both retailers and, it appears, to consumers. "The core town centres are doing fine," says Mr Michael Cooke of the fortnightly magazine *Urban Environment Today*. "But just walk a half mile south, north, east or west and you will see all the dingy back streets that are not getting investment and are suffering." Mr Richard Edwards, retail analyst with brokers Hoare Govett says that the town centre is shrinking. He says retailers are "much more focused about where they want to be because there is less footfall in the high street than there used to be."

It is also still unclear as to the long term impact of electronic commerce on more traditional forms of retailing. Continuing US dominance in the global market for electronic commerce is creating "competitive concerns and some suspicions" in other countries seeking to harness the commercial potential of the Internet, the Organisation for Economic Co-operation and Development has warned. But the OECD says in a report that much of the US lead reflects lags in the growth of the market in Europe and Asia, caused by high costs, slowness to tackle barriers to competition and conservative consumer attitudes. The report also doubts that e-commerce will quickly supplant most traditional forms of retailing or sharply reduce consumer product prices. It finds little evidence that products sold on the Internet are cheaper than those bought at conventional outlets, although there prices change more frequently.[6]

The OECD says the US generated about four fifths of the estimated $26 billion of e-commerce activity in 1997. Although some forecasts suggest the market could be worth $1,000 billion by 2005, the report expects the US share not to fall below two thirds of the total in the near term. It says high telecommunications costs, slow liberalisation and insufficient transmission bandwidth may continue to inhibit development of e-commerce in Europe and Asia. European consumers were also less used to 'distance shopping' than those in the US, where mail order sales per head were more than twice as high. Although the report says the growth of e-commerce will have a big impact in certain sectors, such as financial services, postal services and travel agents, it expects its overall consequences for consumer industries and employment to be limited in the foreseeable future. Even on the most optimistic forecasts, the value of e-commerce transactions worldwide would be smaller in 2005 than direct marketing sales in the US today. The market would also consist overwhelmingly of dealings between businesses, rather than of retail transactions involving consumers. The report concludes that "while the appeal of convenience and mass customisation may promote business-to-consumer e-commerce, its success is not assured. It may become just another channel for retailers, like mail order, rather than a new dominant mode of commerce." Even the strongest advocates of online shopping acknowledge that traditional forms of retailing are not going to go away. "People like the experience of shopping," says Mr Herb Stephens of Intershop, a software company that builds the programs needed to create an e-commerce web site.

Davidson Pavitt, Vice President of Gemini Consulting, predicts a major increase in electronic home shopping via the television and the Internet over the next ten years. Pavitt considers the creation of a 'super high street' an inevitability. He believes that "even if poor delivery mechanisms and consumer concerns about the invasion of their privacy curtail the development of the electronic home shopping industry, they will certainly not stop it in its tracks."[7] So where does this leave traditional retailing? According to Pavitt, it is likely to see changes on at least three fronts: in the nature of the product offerings, customer buying patterns and its place in the value chain. Whatever the response of traditional methods of retailing to the threat of the 'super high street' it seems doomed to failure. As Pavitt says, "these issues will only affect the timing of the transition, for it is not a question of whether, but when, the online retailing revolution occurs. Electronic home shopping is already on the menu, albeit in a limited format. As consumers look for increasingly à la carte products, so they will take to the 'super high street' in their droves."[8]

The *British Shops and Stores Association Yearbook* believes "more retailers try to shape their future than leave it to chance. The design industry is a good example. Every year, designers set out to design next season's fashion. Every year, buyers for clothing retailers also attempt to predict which styles will sell. Attempting to foresee the future, based on experience and vision is essential."[9] This gift of prophecy is important to all retailers who should set out where they want to be in the future and prepare by asking themselves what is our market, who are our customers, competitors and suppliers and what will they be like in the next century? What complicates the planning process is the fact that customers themselves do not necessarily know what they will want in the future.

Bratland considers the benefits of Electronic Data Interchange (EDI) and other electronic developments embraced willingly by retailers. Other challenges to retailers include the expansion into retailing of big companies more renowned in other sectors. An example quoted is in the area of petrol stations, and here it is considered likely that developments will continue through franchising. Franchising enables a greater focus on the retail market, provides finance for expansion and makes it easier to introduce uniform products. If retailers are to take control of the future, they have to shift their focus to the values of the customers, taking note of the developments in the human environment. An example of how customer priorities are driving the industry is the recent opening of the 'Out of This World' store in Bristol. The shop will only sell products that satisfy a set of ethical conditions: not tested on animals; not considered damaging to the environment; and not containing artificial additives. The shop is the first of a chain of 200 such stores planned around the country.

Some trends are, to a degree, out of the control of retailers, but this is even more reason why they should be aware of them and prepared to work with the consequences. Tighter government regulations, for example, are limiting obvious methods of expansion for retailers whilst raising barriers to the creation of further opportunities; planning for further out-of-town centres has stopped; a rejuvenation of the high street has been called for; EC trade barriers have been removed; trading hours have been extended; and changes have occurred in both price fixing legislation and employee working patterns. The challenge for retailers in the future is to keep one step ahead of a fast-moving and often unpredictable market.

In conclusion, we should ask the question – are supermarkets a blessing or a curse? Apart from driving hundreds of small shops out of business, they are thought by many to have become too powerful. According to a recent report commissioned by the government it seems that supermarkets do not benefit society. In this report, CB Hillier Parker, the consultancy firm, argues that the advent of superstores on the edge of towns has ruined town centres, killing off 13-50% of local foodstores as well as many of the local suppliers who depend on those stores. It is the supermarkets' drive to destroy the small trader, says the philosopher Roger Scruton in *The Times*, that has caused many of our modern malaises: "the decline of inner cities, the ruination of the countryside, the collapse of the rural economy and the mania for road-building." Scruton lays the blame fairly and squarely with the local authorities. This is "what happens when local authorities bow to the needs of supermarkets and disregard those of the local ratepayer. It is *local authorities* which grant planning permission and which build access roads to superstores while failing to provide car parking space for those who might otherwise shop in the town centre."

References

1   Koranteng J, *International Online Services: Future Challenges Facing the Consumer and Business Markets* – London: FT Media & Telecoms Publishing, 1997.

2   Groom B, & Jones S , "Out-of-town shopping malls still centres of controversy", *Financial Times*, 10/9/98.

3   Monbiot G, "Superstores for suckers", *The Guardian*, 24/9/98.

4   Jowit J, "Retail capital of the west in fight to re-establish its brand", *Financial Times*, 28/9/98.

5   Hollinger P, "High streets on upward curve", *Financial Times*, 15/3/97.

6   OECD, The economic and social impact of electronic commerce, Paris,1998.

7   Pavitt D, Retailing and the super high street: the future of the electronic home shopping industry, *International Journal of Retail & Distribution Management*, Vol.25, no.1, p38–43, 1997.

8   ibid.

9   Bratland B, The Future of Retailing, *British Shops and Stores Association Yearbook*, 1996, p15–17.

Appendix – Useful organisations

Association of Town Centre Management
1 Queen Anne's Gate,
London SW1H 9BT
Tel: 0171 222 0120
Fax: 0171 222 4440

British Franchise Association
Thames View,
Newtown Road,
Henley-on-Thames,
Oxfordshire RG9 1HG
Tel: 01491 578050
Fax: 01491 573517

British Institute of Retailing
66-68 College Road,
Harrow,
Middlesex HA1 1FD
Tel: 0181 324 1609
Fax: 0181 324 1235

British Shops and Stores Association
Middleton House,
2 Main Road,
Banbury,
Oxfordshire OX17 2TN
Tel: 01295 712277
Fax: 01295 711665

British Retail Consortium (BRC)
5 Grafton Street,
London W1X 3LB
Tel: 0171 647 1500
Fax: 0171 647 1599

CB Hillier Parker
77 Grosvenor Street,
London W1A 2BT
Tel: 0171 629 7666
Fax: 0171 409 3016

Centre for Retail Studies
The John Henry Newman Building,
University College Dublin,
Belfield,
Dublin 4,
Ireland
Tel: 0353 1 706 8426
Fax: 0353 1 269 5597

Corporate Intelligence on Retailing
51 Doughty Street,
London WC1N 2LS
Tel: 0171 696 9006
Fax: 0171 696 9004

Datamonitor
106 Baker Street,
London W1M 1LA
Tel: 0171 625 8548
Fax: 0171 625 5080

Euromonitor
60–61 Britton Street,
London EC1M 5NA
Tel: 0171 251 8024
Fax: 0171 608 3149

Healey & Baker
29 St George Street,
Hanover Square,
London W1A 3BG
Tel: 0171 629 9292
Fax: 0171 514 2360

Institute for Public Policy Research (IPPR)
30–32 Southampton Street,
London WC2E 7RA
Tel: 0171 379 9400
Fax: 0171 497 0373

Institute for Retail Studies
University of Stirling,
Stirling FK9 4LA
Tel: 01786 467386
Fax: 01786 465290

Institute of Grocery Distribution (IGD)
Letchmore Heath,
Watford WD2 8DQ
Tel: 01923 857141
Fax: 01923 852531

International Council of Shopping Centres (ICSC)
665 5th Avenue,
New York, NY 10022,
USA
Tel: (212) 421 8181
Fax: (212) 486 0849

Key Note
Field House,
72 Oldfield Road,
Hampton,
Middlesex TW12 2HQ
Tel: 0181 783 0755
Fax: 0181 783 0049

Lafferty Publications
7th Floor,
IDA House,
Pearse Street,
Dublin 2,
Ireland
Tel: 0353 1 718022
Fax: 0353 1 718240

Management Horizons Europe
Waverley House,
Lower Square,
Isleworth,
Middlesex TW7 6RL
Tel: 0181 560 9393
Fax: 0181 568 6900

Market Assessment (MAPS)
Field House,
72 Oldfield Road,
Hampton,
Middlesex TW12 2HQ
Tel: 0181 481 8710
Fax: 0181 783 0310

Mintel International Group Ltd
18-19 Long Lane,
London EC1A 9HE
Tel: 0171 606 6000
Fax: 0171 606 5932

Newman Books
32 Vauxhall Bridge Road,
London SW1V 2YY
Tel: 0171 973 6402
Fax: 0171 233 5057

NTC Publications
Farm Road,
Henley-on-Thames,
Oxon RG9 1EJ
Tel: 01491 574671
Fax: 01491 571188

OECD
2 rue André-Pascal,
75775 Paris Cedex 16,
France
Tel: 033 1 45 24 82 00

Oxford Institute of Retail Management (OXIRM)
Templeton College,
Kennington Road,
Kennington,
Oxfordshire OX1 5NY
Tel: 01865 735422
Fax: 01865 736374

Unit for Retail Planning Information (URPI)
7 Southern Court,
South Street,
Reading RG1 4QS
Tel: 0118 958 8181
Fax: 0118 959 7637

Urban and Economic Development Group (URBED)
41 Old Birley Street,
Manchester M16 5RF
Tel: 0161 226 5078
Fax: 0161 226 7307

Verdict Research
112 High Holborn,
London WC1V 6JS
Tel: 0171 404 5042
Fax: 0171 430 0059

Index

A

airport retailing 83
Asda 156
Association of Town Centre Managers
   166

B

Bluewater 51-52
Boots the Chemist 63-64
British Council of Shopping Centres
   68
British Retail Consortium (BRC) v,
   vii, 83

C

category killers 102
CB Hillier Parker 43, 55, 103, 172
convenience retailing 93-95, 113
cross-border retailing 106
customer loyalty 91-93

D

Datamonitor 95, 128

E

efficient consumer response (ECR)
   87-88
electronic commerce 86-89, 107, 109-
   110, 119-121, 125, 127, 131-133,
   153-157, 164-166, 170
electronic data interchange (EDI) 85-
   87, 131-132, 171
electronic point-of-sale (EPoS) 88-90
employment 73
environment 64-65
Euromonitor 69-70, 90

F

financial services 79, 95-96, 129-131,
   140-141, 154
forecourt retailing 105
franchising 82

G

Goad, Charles 70
government policy 4-7, 10, 16, 20-22,
   25-27, 30, 59-61,169
Gummer, John 5-6, 20, 50-52, 61, 167

H

Healey and Baker 39, 57, 103-104,
   111, 123
home shopping 108, 122-123, 127,
   133, 140, 143-149, 156-158

I

Iceland 149
Institute for Public Policy Research
   (IPPR) 15
Institute of Grocery Distribution
   (IGD) 20, 88-89
intelligent agents 124-125
International Council of Shopping
   Centres (ICSC) 81
internationalisation 83, 106
Internet 120-121, 124-125, 128-139,
   142-159, 164-166, 170

K

Key Note 84

THE BRITISH LIBRARY

THE INSTANT GUIDE TO COMPANY INFORMATION ONLINE - EUROPE
by Nigel Spencer, 3rd edition

Looking for company information in computer databases and on the World Wide Web? A new edition of a popular British Library guide can help you get there faster.

Written by an experienced business information searcher, *The Instant Guide* presents, for each featured European country, lists of relevant databases, showing for each of them:

- language
- which online hosts offer access
- the number of companies covered
- whether certain categories of information are available, such as employee numbers and sales
- whether these categories can be used as search criteria (eg can you search for companies which are exporters?)

There is also a table covering pan-European databases together with an A-Z list of databases, address and contact details for the various online hosts/services, and a separate section on the World Wide Web, giving selected Websites which provide company information, often free of charge. A final section describes the range of company types in each European country and the published data available for each type.

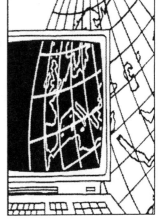

Reference Reviews described the first edition as "an ingenious production, and one that will be welcomed by business information officers and librarians". With new coverage of selected Central and Eastern European countries including the Czech Republic, Poland, Slovakia and the Ukraine, as well as new material on the World Wide Web, this third edition of *The Instant Guide* is the best yet. At £37 it is an essential purchase for researchers and consultants, business libraries and information centres, other advice centres such as Business Links, and for the producers and publishers of business databases. People running their own businesses who need to find out about other companies, as suppliers, customers or competitors, will also find it invaluable.

1999, 84 pages, 297x210mm, paperback
Key Resource series, ISBN 0-7123-0846-6
Price £37 (UK postage included, overseas postage extra)

By the same author:

News Information: Online, CD-ROM and Internet Resources lists news online and CD-ROM databases by region and country and provides URLs for the Websites of specific newspapers and other news-based sites. Focusing on commercial and economic news as well as current affairs, *News Information* will be of particular value to business information officers and commercial researchers, as well as journalists.

1997, 72 pages, 297x210mm, paperback
Key Resource series, ISBN 0-7123-0833-4
Price £37 (UK postage included, overseas postage extra)

Orders to: British Library section, Turpin Distribution Services Ltd, Blackhorse Road, Letchworth, Herts SG6 1HN, UK. Tel 01462 672555, Fax 01462 480947, E-mail turpin@rsc.org
Please make cheques payable to the British Library.

Orders for the USA and Canada to: University of Toronto Press, 5201 Dufferin Street, Downsview, Ontario, M3H 5T8 Canada. Tel 416 667 7791, Fax 416 667 7832.

THE BRITISH LIBRARY

Science, Technology and Business publications

The British Library has one of the world's outstanding reference collections in science and technology, social science, medicine, business and patents. The Library is committed to making this information available to as wide an audience as possible.

With its own list, and in association with a growing list of other publishers, the British Library produces a wide range of publications designed to serve the information needs of scientists, librarians, researchers and business people. The list includes books, journals and CD-ROMs.

If you would like a free copy of our catalogue of science, technology and business publications please contact

Paul Wilson
The British Library
Publications Office
96 Euston Road
London NW1 2DB

Tel 020-7412 7472
Fax 020-7412 7768
E-mail paul.wilson@bl.uk